Frank Heinlein
Residentials by Werner Sobek

**av**edition

Dédié à mon ami Jacques Barrot, un grand européen.
1937–2014

Table of Contents
Inhaltsverzeichnis

| | | |
|---|---|---|
| Table of Contents | Inhaltsverzeichnis | 004 |
| Preface | Vorwort | 006 |
| Introduction | Einführung | 008 |
| R128, Stuttgart | R128, Stuttgart | 016 |
| H16, Tieringen | H16, Tieringen | 034 |
| S3, Southern Germany | S3, Süddeutschland | 048 |
| D10, Biberach | D10, Biberach | 060 |
| F87, Berlin | F87, Berlin | 078 |
| R6, Königswinter | R6, Königswinter | 094 |
| Y1, Yssingeaux | Y1, Yssingeaux | 110 |
| Aktivhaus B10, Stuttgart | Aktivhaus B10, Stuttgart | 124 |
| Interview with Werner Sobek | Gespräch mit Werner Sobek | 146 |
| Imprint | Impressum | 160 |

Preface
*Vorwort*

Our built environment must not only be sustainable, but also breathtakingly beautiful – this challenge represents a central element of Werner Sobek's work. On his path to achieving this goal, the architect, engineer and researcher from Stuttgart has continually designed experimental structures that exemplify the quintessence of his thought. In Sobek's buildings, functionality, aesthetics and user comfort are always regarded as parts of a whole. Nowhere is this concept more impressively illustrated than in his single-family homes. This type of building therefore provides the focus of this book, which presents a selection of structures from the past two decades. An introduction by and an interview with Werner Sobek round off this very personal insight into his intellectual and professional world.

Unsere gebaute Umwelt muss nicht nur nachhaltig, sondern auch atemberaubend schön sein – so eine zentrale Forderung von Werner Sobek. Auf dem Weg zu diesem Ziel entwirft der Stuttgarter Architekt, Ingenieur und Forscher immer wieder Experimentalbauten, die beispielhaft für die Quintessenz seines Denkens sind. Funktionalität, Ästhetik und Nutzerkomfort werden bei diesen Bauten immer als Teil eines Ganzen betrachtet. Besonders beeindruckend wird dies bei Werner Sobeks Einfamilienhäusern deutlich. Auf diesem Gebäudetypus liegt deshalb auch der Fokus des vorliegenden Buchs, das ausgewählte Bauwerke aus den vergangenen zwei Jahrzehnten präsentiert. Ein einführender Text von und ein Interview mit Werner Sobek runden diesen sehr persönlichen Einblick in seine Denk- und Arbeitswelt ab.

Frank Heinlein

Introduction  
Einführung

How to Build in the Future?
We are striving after a form of architecture that is equal to the challenges of our time. A form of architecture that is mindful of the way it reflects our responsibility towards our children. Such architecture must have a positive relationship with the natural world, its users and new technologies. Backward thinking – be it ecological, aesthetic or technological – can and should no longer be justified by a need for continuity or the legitimacy of falling back on tried-and-tested methods. Instead, we must draw a distinction between that which can be deemed adequate, reliable, even 'correct' in a wider temporal context, and that comfortable convenience which allows many design concepts, construction techniques and materials to see continued use long after they have become obsolete and no longer suitable for the present day.

A form of architecture which can claim to have developed an approach that befits both the present and the future age must arise from a foundation of integral planning and organisational processes and the radical application of ecological considerations. The question is not 'how have we lived and worked in the past?', but 'how can we and how do we want to live and work in the future?' Faced with the imperative for sustainable construction, however, we need also ask: 'how must we build in the years to come?'

Wie weiter bauen?
Wir streben nach einer Architektur, die den Herausforderungen unserer Zeit gerecht wird und die sich als Spiegel der Verantwortung gegenüber unseren Kindern versteht. Eine solche Architektur muss ein positives Verhältnis zur natürlichen Umwelt, zu ihren Nutzern und zu neuen Technologien haben. Ökologische, ästhetische oder technologische Rückständigkeit kann und darf nicht länger aus einem Bedarf an Kontinuität oder aus der Legitimität des Rückgriffs auf Bewährtes begründet werden. Stattdessen gilt es zu trennen zwischen dem, was als angemessen, bewährt, vielleicht sogar als „richtig" in einem größeren zeitlichen Rahmen bezeichnet werden kann, und der Bequemlichkeit, die viele längst überholte und nicht mehr zeitgerechte Gestaltungskonzeptionen, Bautechniken und Materialien weiterhin zum Einsatz kommen lässt.

Eine Architektur, die den Anspruch besitzt, eine unserer und der kommenden Zeit angemessene Haltung zu formulieren, muss auf der Basis integraler Planungs- und Organisationsprozesse sowie einer radikalen Umsetzung ökologischer Überlegungen entstehen. Die Frage lautet nicht „Wie haben wir gewohnt und gearbeitet?", sondern „Wie können und wie wollen wir künftig wohnen und arbeiten?" Aber sie lautet angesichts des Imperativs des nachhaltigen Bauens auch: „Wie müssen wir zukünftig bauen?"

Answering these questions requires the anticipation of the future. Like all forward thinking, this approach is always afflicted with the risk of error and the chance of heading in the wrong direction from time to time. The prospect of going astray must not discourage such thought, however: its intellectual tenability makes it the only possible path ahead. In other words – to use a dictum from Georg Wilhelm Friedrich Hegel's 'Phenomenology of Spirit' – '... the fear of making a mistake is a mistake in itself.' The applicability of this statement remains undiminished to this day.

Around two billion people under the age of 16 currently exist on our planet. Although they are still living 'at home', they will require housing, workplaces and an infrastructure to be built for them over the next 16 years. As a consequence we must, in this short period of time, expand today's built environment by the same number of structures that existed in total around the year 1930 (when the Earth's entire population only amounted to approximately 2 billion individuals). The impossibility of this task is only now slowly dawning on most people. Faced with this situation, we designers must ask ourselves what the construction industry can or must do to absorb the resulting ecological and social upheaval that threatens to take place. How can our built environment consume fewer fossil fuels and other resources? How can it produce less waste? It is vital

Die Antwort hierauf bedingt die Antizipation des Kommenden – ein wie jedes Nachdenken über die Zukunft immer mit der Gefahr von Irrtümern behaftetes, hie und da vielleicht sogar in die falsche Richtung führendes Vorgehen. Die Gefahr des Irrens darf aber nicht von derartigem Denken abhalten, weist es doch hinsichtlich seiner intellektuellen Vertretbarkeit den einzig möglichen Weg. Oder, anders ausgedrückt: Das von Georg Wilhelm Friedrich Hegel in seiner „Phänomenologie des Geistes" geprägte Diktum „... dass die Furcht zu irren schon der Irrtum selbst ist" gilt noch immer mit uneingeschränkter Wirkung.

Heute leben ca. zwei Milliarden Menschen auf der Erde, die jünger als 16 Jahre sind. Für diese heute noch „zu Hause" lebenden Menschen gilt es, in den kommenden 16 Jahren Wohnungen, Arbeitsplätze und eine Infrastruktur zu bauen. Das bedeutet, dass wir in dieser kurzen Zeitspanne die gesamte gebaute Umwelt, wie sie um 1930 bestand (als insgesamt nur ca. 2 Milliarden Menschen auf der Erde lebten), noch einmal bauen müssen. Die Unmöglichkeit dieser Aufgabe wird den meisten erst langsam bewusst. Angesichts dieser Entwicklung müssen wir als Planer fragen, was das Bauschaffen tun kann oder muss, um die aus dieser Entwicklung drohenden ökologischen und sozialen Verwerfungen abzufedern.

that these questions be answered as a matter of urgency if we want to shape our world in a way that meets the needs of the future.

We have dedicated ourselves to these questions in our own work for nearly 20 years. In doing so, our search for what should and could exist the day after tomorrow has developed a much greater scope. It not only includes research into the minimal, but also the intangible, the temporary, and the ephemeral. It enquires into forms of living and working in the metropolis (the ultimate density environment), in movement, underwater and in the extra-terrestrial realm. It features our own research and development surrounding such issues as recyclable construction, self-learning home automation systems, and the development of smart grids. It involves both visual and non-visual architecture – that is the architecture of the unseen, the architectural experience that emerges through tactile perception, the sense of smell, acoustic awareness, and the consciousness of currents of heat and air. We are constantly 'fathoming the depths' and seeking out the boundaries – after all, only those who know where the boundaries are can overstep them in search of other forms of living and working, other building technologies and other methods of managing our habitats.

Wie kann unsere gebaute Umwelt weniger fossile Brennstoffe und sonstige Ressourcen verbrauchen? Wie kann sie weniger Abfälle erzeugen? Diese Fragen müssen zwingend und in naher Zukunft beantwortet werden, wenn wir unsere Welt zukunftsgerecht gestalten wollen.

In unserem eigenen Schaffen widmen wir uns den genannten Fragen seit nahezu 20 Jahren. Unsere Suche nach dem, was übermorgen sein sollte und könnte, greift dabei weit aus. Sie umfasst die Erforschung des Minimalen genauso wie die des Immateriellen, des Temporären, des Ephemeren. Sie fragt nach den Formen des Wohnens und Arbeitens in der maximalen Verdichtung, der Metropole, in der Bewegung, unter Wasser oder im extraterrestrischen Raum. Sie umfasst eigene Forschungs- und Entwicklungsarbeiten zu Themen wie dem recyclinggerechten Bauen, selbstlernenden Hausautomationssystemen oder der Entwicklung von Smart Grids. Sie umfasst die visuelle wie die nichtvisuelle Architektur, also die Architektur des Nichtsichtbaren, die Architekturerfahrung, die durch die Tastsinne, das Riechen, die akustische Wahrnehmung, die Wahrnehmung von Wärme- und Luftströmungen entsteht. Stets geht es uns dabei um „Auslotungen", um die Suche nach den Grenzen. Denn: Nur wer die Grenzen kennt, kann sie überschreiten – in Richtung anderer Formen des Wohnens und Arbeitens, anderer Technologien des Bauens und anderer Methoden des Betreibens unserer Habitate.

An important part of our work in this respect is represented by the houses we design. Since the turn of the millennium, we have planned and built an average of one house a year to serve as a vehicle for future development. Naturally, these houses must also be suitable for inhabitation and use. These buildings have initially been 'small' in size. This in no way means that we regard single-family homes as a particularly important form of construction, however. Rather, the buildings are small because it allows us to minimise the innovation-related risk for all parties involved. Our developments are always designed for implementation on a large scale, be that in high-rise or high-density buildings or built for a high or low price bracket. These 'small' projects allow us to study the usefulness of our developments and utilise the experience gained to either improve our approaches step by step – or discard them altogether. The present book displays selected works from this developmental series.

When we started work, we made the radical call to depart from a trend that aimed to minimise the energy consumed over a building's service life by using ever-smaller windows and increasingly well insulated, airtight rooms. We demanded the exact opposite: the greatest possible transparency combined with the Triple Zero© principle (no use of fossilised energy sources; no emissions; no residual waste during

Einen wichtigen Teil unserer diesbezüglichen Arbeiten stellen die von uns geplanten Häuser dar. Seit der Jahrtausendwende planen und entwickeln wir im Durchschnitt jedes Jahr ein Haus, das als Entwicklungsträger dient, trotzdem aber natürlich bewohnbar, benutzbar sein muss. Diese Gebäude sind zunächst einmal „klein" – was aber keineswegs bedeutet, dass wir Einfamilienhäuser als eine besonders wichtige Bauform ansehen. Die Gebäude sind deshalb klein, weil wir damit das Entwicklungsrisiko für alle Beteiligten minimieren können. Ausgelegt sind diese Entwicklungen aber stets für eine Anwendung im „Großen", sei es im Hochhausbau oder im stark Verdichteten, sei es im Niedrig- oder im Hochpreisniveau. An unseren „kleinen" Objekten können wir die Sinnhaftigkeit unserer Entwicklungen studieren und unsere Ansätze dann, darauf aufbauend, Schritt für Schritt verbessern – oder verwerfen. Das vorliegende Buch zeigt ausgewählte Arbeiten aus dieser Entwicklungsreihe auf.

Am Anfang unserer Arbeiten stand die radikale Forderung nach der Abkehr von dem Trend, ein „Weniger" an Energieverbrauch in der Nutzungsphase mit immer kleineren Fenstern, immer mehr Dämmung sowie die Luftdichtigkeit der Räume zu erreichen. Wir forderten geradezu das Gegenteil: Weitestgehende Transparenz, verbunden mit dem Triple

dismantling or conversion). R128 was our first solution. Thereafter followed many important buildings, including D10 (which generated approximately 130% of the energy it required for its own needs), F87 (170%), and Aktivhaus B10 (200%). Our work on R128 set new standards in the reduction of resource consumption – the building weighed a mere sixth of a house of the same size built with a conventional load-bearing construction. Moreover, R128 is fully recyclable – a goal pursued in our work since 1992. R128 was the first time widespread awareness was generated for the essential need to have a recyclable built environment. The approaches, design principles, and technologies we developed for this structure have proven very important for numerous further projects.

Recyclability, zero emissions and the reduction of resource consumption have all formed cornerstones of our work from the beginning. The continual progress made in our projects has set the bar increasingly high for new work while always retaining the same basic principles. Our handling of the energy efficiency of buildings has certainly changed time and again as the years have passed, however. On one hand, we have oscillated between minimising energy consumption and maximising in-house energy generation. On the other, we have striven to meet Zero©-Prinzip (kein Verbrauch fossiler Energieträger, keine Emissionen, keine Rückstände bei Ab- oder Umbau). R128 war unsere erste Antwort. Darauf folgten viele wichtige Gebäude wie z. B. D10 (das ca.130 % der benötigten Energie selbst erzeugt), F87 (170 %) oder Aktivhaus B10 (200 %). Mit R128 haben wir neue Maßstäbe in der Reduktion des Ressourcenverbrauchs gesetzt – das Haus wiegt gerade einmal 1/6 des Gewichts eines in herkömmlicher Massivbauweise gebauten Hauses gleicher Größe. R128 ist zudem vollkommen rezyklierbar – ein in unseren Arbeiten seit 1992 verfolgter Aspekt. Mit R128 gelang es erstmals, in großer Breite ein Bewusstsein für die Notwendigkeit der Rezyklierbarkeit der gebauten Umwelt zu schaffen. Die von uns hierzu entwickelten Ansätze, Entwurfsprinzipien und Technologien waren sehr wichtig für viele weitere Projekte

Die Reduzierung des Verbrauchs von Ressourcen war genauso wie Rezyklierbarkeit und Emissionsfreiheit von Anfang an Grundlage unserer Arbeit. Die bei unseren Projekten kontinuierlich erzielten Fortschritte schufen ein zunehmend höheres Ausgangsniveau für neue Arbeiten, haben aber den Grundansatz stets bewahrt. Unser Umgang mit der energetischen Effizienz von Gebäuden hat sich allerdings in den vergangenen Jahren immer wieder verändert. Dabei ging es zum einen um das

the requirement of creating a Zero- or Plus-Energy house based not on annual results but on ever-shorter reporting periods. Although R128's seasonal variations between energy surplus and shortfall are balanced out when viewed over the space of a year, they are nevertheless very high in absolute terms. These levels were already significantly reduced in projects as early as H16 and D10, and an annual surplus of 170 % was achieved with only moderate fluctuations in F87. Ultimately, B10 saw us attain an annual energy surplus of 200 % with even smaller disparities.

Aktivhaus B10 and its predecessors have allowed us to codify design approaches, construction methods and technologies on the basis of which further structures – multi-storey residences, houses in other climate zones, homes for low-salary groups, etc. – can now be produced. With all of these buildings, we will continually strive to answer the questions that drive us: 'how can we create an architecture that befits both the present and the future?', and 'how shall we live tomorrow?'

Pendeln zwischen einer Minimierung des Energieverbrauchs und einer Maximierung der hauseigenen Energieerzeugung. Zum anderen ging es um das Bestreben, die Forderung nach einem Null- oder Plusenergiehaus nicht auf der Basis der Jahresbilanz, sondern mit immer kürzeren Bilanzierungszeiträumen zu erfüllen. Während sich die saisonalen Schwankungen zwischen Über- und Unterdeckung bei R128 zwar über die Jahresspanne ausgleichen, trotzdem aber sehr hoch sind, wurden sie bereits bei H16 und D10 deutlich reduziert. Bei F87 gelang eine auf das Jahr bezogene Überproduktion von 170 % bei mäßigen Schwankungen, bei B10 schließlich eine auf das Jahr bezogene Überproduktion von 200 % bei noch kleineren Schwankungen.

Mit dem Aktivhaus B10 ebenso wie mit seinen Vorgängerbauten haben wir Gestaltungsansätze, Konstruktionsmethoden und Technologien festgeschrieben, auf deren Basis nun weitere Gebäude entstehen werden. Mehrgeschossige Häuser, Häuser in anderen Klimazonen, Häuser für niedrige Einkommensgruppen und andere. Mit allen diesen Gebäuden versuchen wir weiterhin, Antworten auf die Fragen nach einer der heutigen und der zukünftigen Zeit angemessenen Architektur, nach einem Leben im morgen zu finden.

Werner Sobek

R128, Stuttgart
R128, Stuttgart

R128 was a radical answer to developments in sustainable construction, in particular the Passivhaus ('Passive House') standard which shaped planning culture at the end of the 1990s. Our goal was to break away from the focus on small windows, total airtightness and thick insulation. On the one hand, this was done to demonstrate opportunities for innovation; on the other, it was designed to reverse the trend for an 'aesthetics of asceticism' in construction. R128 does not reduce the transparent proportion of the facade, and instead uses the most up-to-date glazing technologies to create a lifestyle in which complete transparency allows a constant connection with nature and the environment. In R128, one always has 360-degree view – a wide vista which also serves to broaden the soul and the mind. When it rains, water can be seen running down the glass. On winter nights, frost patterns measuring nearly 100 m$^2$ in size emerge on the house's west facade. This transparency allows one to experience the time of day and the seasons much more intensely than in a conventional house. One also has a much stronger relationship with natural light than in a normal building – a factor of great importance for one's sense of wellbeing. Indeed, a Professor of Psychotherapy once remarked that R128 is an antidepressant.

R128 war eine radikale Antwort auf Entwicklungen im nachhaltigen Bauen, speziell im Passivhausbau, wie sie Ende der 1990er-Jahre die Planungskultur prägten. Ziel war, die Fokussierung auf kleine Fensterflächen, absolute Luftdichtigkeit und dicke Wärmedämmpakete aufzubrechen. Zum einen sollten so Innovationsmöglichkeiten aufgezeigt werden; zum anderen ging es um eine Umkehrung des Trends hin zu einer „Entsagungsästhetik" im Bauen. R128 reduziert nicht den transparenten Anteil der Fassade, sondern nutzt vielmehr modernste Verglasungstechnologien, um ein Wohnen in der vollständigen Transparenz, in ständiger Verbindung mit der Natur und der Umwelt zu schaffen. In R128 hat man stets eine Rundumsicht von 360 Grad – der weite Blick weitet auch die geistigen Perspektiven und die Seele. Man sieht bei Regen das Wasser an der Fassade ablaufen. In Winternächten entstehen auf der Außenseite der Westfassade nahezu 100 m$^2$ große Flächen aus Eisblumen. Dank dieser Transparenz ist ein viel intensiveres Erleben der Tages- und der Jahreszeiten möglich als in einem herkömmlichen Haus. Man lebt viel stärker mit dem natürlichen Licht als in einem normalen Gebäude. Dies ist sehr wichtig für das Wohlbefinden. R128 sei ein Antidepressivum, bemerkte einst ein Ordinarius für Psychotherapie.

View of the house from the rear garden – the structure and functionality of the building are instantly visible.
Ansicht des Hauses vom rückwärtigen Garten – Struktur und Funktionalität des Gebäudes erschließen sich auf einen Blick.

R128 stands to the south of Stuttgart on a steep slope with an average incline of 35 degrees. It is framed by a very carefully developed garden which is shaped by strict geometric patterns of non-local plants in the immediate vicinity of the house. The garden's artificial character is based on that of the building itself. The further the garden moves away from the house, the more irregular and feral it becomes, and the more the landscape is filled with indigenous plants. Both the access ways and the upper surface of the terraces consist of metal grating that floats above the natural surroundings at a height of 20 cm. Nature itself is thus as little affected as possible – an embodiment of an approach also made manifest in the fact that R128 has neither a cellar nor any pipes and cables in the ground. Stretching over an elevation of 70 metres and traversed by a meandering pathway, the garden's design is an essential part of the overarching architectural concept. While R128 itself only took ten weeks to build, the garden's sloping location and the growing times of the plants meant that it was nearly 15 years before it assumed its desired form.

R128 was Werner Sobek's first Triple Zero House. It dispenses with energy from fossil fuels, produces no emissions and is fully recyclable. In

R128 steht an einem steilen Hang im Stuttgarter Süden, der eine durchschnittliche Neigung von 35 Grad aufweist. Es wird von einem mit großer Sorgfalt entwickelten Garten eingerahmt, der in der unmittelbaren Umgebung des Hauses durch ortsuntypische Pflanzen in streng geometrischen Mustern geprägt ist. Der Garten orientiert sich mit seinem artifiziellen Charakter am Gebäude selbst. Je weiter sich der Garten vom Gebäude entfernt, desto irregulärer, verwilderter wird er, wobei dabei immer mehr ortstypische Pflanzen das Bild prägen. Die Erschließungswege zum Haus wie die Oberflächen der Terrassen bestehen aus metallischen Gitterrosten, die in 20 cm Höhe über der Natur schweben. Die Natur wird also möglichst wenig berührt – Ausdruck einer Haltung, die sich auch in der Tatsache manifestiert, dass R128 keinen Keller hat und dass es keinerlei im Boden befindliche Leitungen gibt. Die Gestaltung des sich über 70 Höhenmeter erstreckenden Gartens, der von einem mäandrierenden Weg durchzogen wird, ist wesentlicher Bestandteil des architektonischen Gesamtkonzepts. Während die Bauzeit für R128 zehn Wochen betrug, benötigte der Garten aufgrund der Hanglage und der Wachstumszeiten der Pflanzen nahezu 15 Jahre, bis er die angestrebte Form einnahm.

The house is accessed via a simple, elegant raised walkway. Connected to the upper storey, it offers an impressive view of Stuttgart's valley basin.

Der Zugang zum Haus erfolgt über einen filigranen Steg, der an das oberste Geschoss anschließt und einen beeindruckenden Ausblick auf den Stuttgarter Talkessel bietet.

Overleaf: Steel frame, bracing, internal developement, ceilings and flooring.

Nächste Seite: Stahlskelett, Aussteifungen, interne Erschließung, Decken und Boden.

addition, R128 represents an extremely sparing approach to resources, as its total weight (from the upper edge of the foundations) amounts to just 39 metric tonnes – a mere sixth of the weight of a conventionally built house of the same size. R128's loadbearing construction consists of a steel skeleton into which strong, 60 mm laminated wooden floor panels have been inserted. These flooring panels can be taken out at anytime and installed elsewhere. The ceilings are formed using a total of 160 aluminium elements. All of these elements are equipped with hand holes for fitting and removal, integrated lights, pre-stamped sound absorbing surfaces and heat/cooling registers. The facade consists of triple glazing with a noble gas filling (krypton) and has a U-value (thermal transmittance coefficient) of 0.44 $W/(m^2 \cdot K)$. The central layer of the triple glazing consists of a thin, coated synthetic film. The entire facade hangs from the roof construction over four floors, allowing distortions between the building and the glass to be compensated for. At the time of its installation, the facade technology designed for R128 had never been used anywhere else in the world – leading to some manufacturers declining to give warranties or guarantees for their products.

R128 uses a very simple heating and cooling concept. In essence, this consists of a closed stream of water that circulates through copper

R128 war Werner Sobeks erstes Triple-Zero-Haus. Es verbraucht keine fossile Energie mehr, erzeugt keine Emissionen und ist vollkommen rezyklierbar. R128 steht zudem für einen äußerst sparsamen Umgang mit den Ressourcen, denn es wiegt mit einem Gesamtgewicht (ab Oberkante Fundament) von 39 Tonnen gerade einmal 1/6 des Gewichts eines in herkömmlicher Bauweise errichteten Hauses gleicher Größe. Die tragende Konstruktion von R128 besteht aus einem Stahlskelett, in das 60 mm starke Bodenelemente aus Dickholz eingelegt sind. Die Bodenelemente lassen sich jederzeit herausnehmen und an anderer Stelle wieder einbauen. Die Deckenuntersichten werden durch insgesamt 160 Aluminiumelemente gebildet. Jedes dieser Elemente besitzt Handlöcher für die Montage bzw. Demontage, integrierte Leuchten, eine eingestanzte Schallabsorberfläche sowie Heiz-Kühl-Register. Die Fassade besteht aus einer Dreifachverglasung mit Kryptonfüllung (Edelgas) und besitzt einen U-Wert (Wärmedurchgangskoeffizient) von 0,44 $W/(m^2 \cdot K)$. Die mittlere Lage der Dreifachverglasung besteht dabei aus einer dünnen, beschichteten Kunststofffolie. Die gesamt Fassade hängt über vier Geschosse von der Dachkonstruktion ab, wodurch Verformungen zwischen dem Gebäude und der Verglasung kompensiert werden können. Die für R128 konzipierte Fassadentechnologie galt zum Zeitpunkt ihres Einbaus als

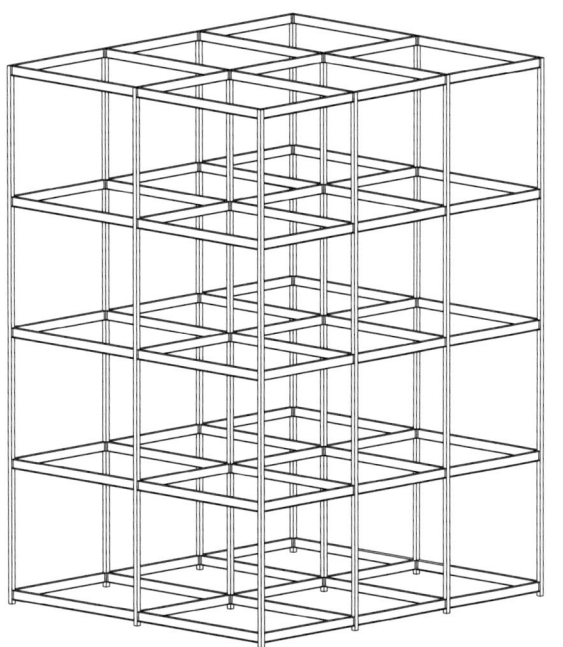
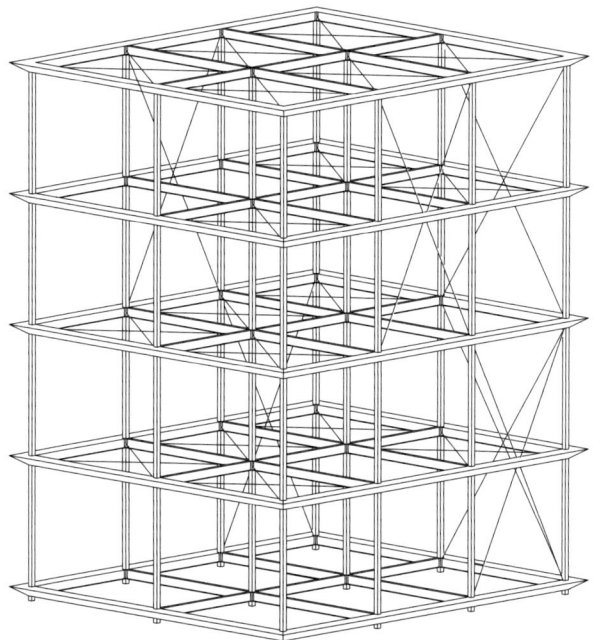

022/023
R 128, Stuttgart

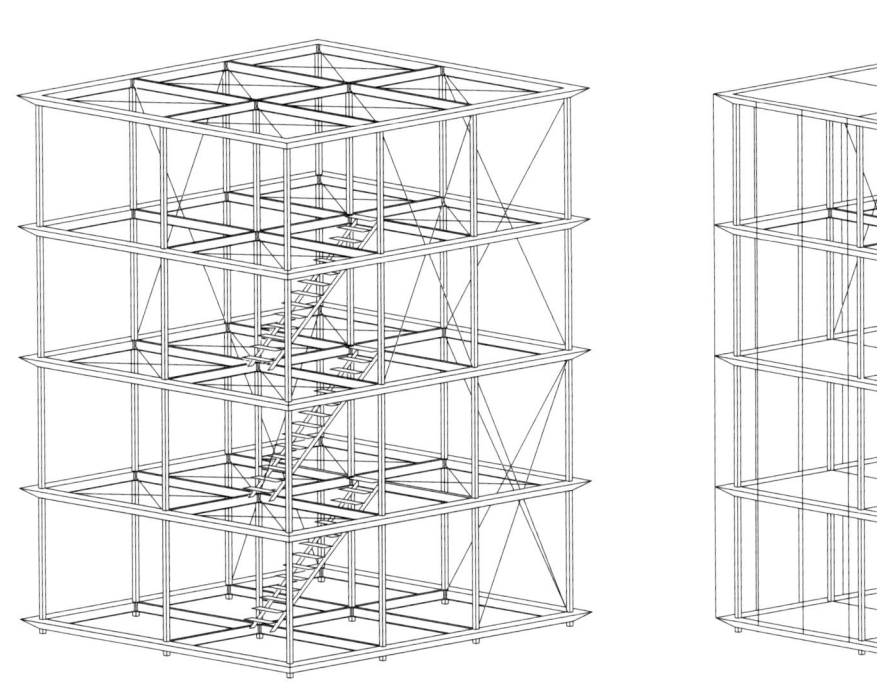
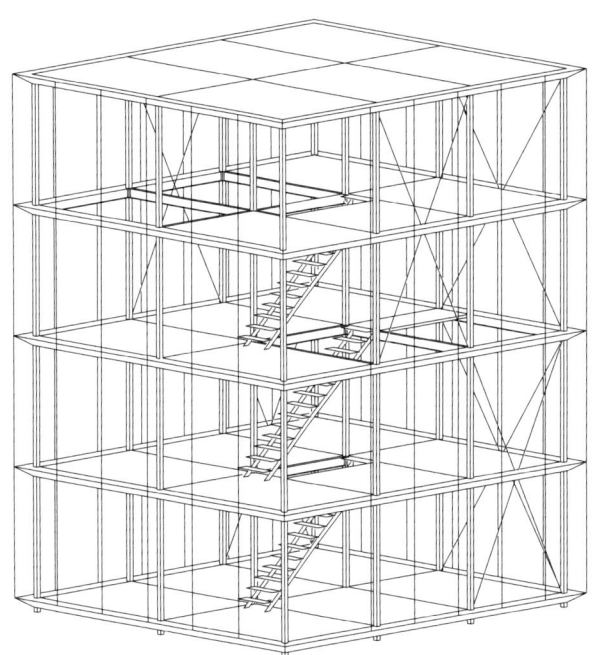

The house, which nestles into the green hills of Stuttgart, offers a breath-taking view of the city below.
Eingebettet in die grünen Hänge Stuttgarts, bietet das Haus einen atemberaubenden Ausblick auf die Stadt zu seinen Füßen.
Overleaf: The building's transparency and openness create numerous horizontal and vertical lines of sight.
Nächste Seite: Die Transparenz und Offenheit des Gebäudes ermöglicht zahlreiche horizontale und vertikale Blickbezüge.

pipes in the ceiling. These pipes also serve as a heat or cooling register. Cold water runs through them in summer to cool the building. Thermal gains are introduced into a water tank located within the house via a heat exchanger. This water tank, enclosed in approx. 400 mm of insulation, has a volume of around 12,000 litres. When heating is required, the process is reversed: warm water from the tank is fed through the ceiling elements, ensuring a pleasant interior temperature.

R128 is an almost fully recyclable building. All of the structural components were produced as single-material parts. The connections between these individual elements are user-friendly and standardised, meaning that the assembly of a building such as R128 can be carried out in around 10 days. Disassembling the building and splitting it into separate groups of individual, homogeneous component parts only requires as little as two to three days. Particular attention was paid to recyclability during the design and planning stages. R128 was intended to provide an example of how it is possible to completely reconceptualise the (temporary) use of resources in the construction industry – an idea that appears time and again in later houses.

weltweit erste Anwendung – was dazu führte, dass einige der Hersteller keine Gewährleistung bzw. Garantien auf ihre Produkte gaben.

R128 verfügt über ein sehr einfaches Heiz-Kühl-Konzept. Dieses besteht im Wesentlichen darin, dass in einem geschlossenen Kreislauf Wasser durch die Kupferrohre in der Decke strömt. Diese Rohre dienen also als Heiz- bzw. als Kühlregister. Im Sommer werden sie von kaltem Wasser durchströmt. Das Gebäude wird so gekühlt; thermische Gewinne werden über einen Wärmetauscher in einen im Haus befindlichen Wassertank eingeleitet. Dieser mit ca. 400 mm Isolierung umgebene Wassertank hat ein Volumen von ca. 12.000 Litern. Im Heizungsfall wird der Prozess umgekehrt, das heißt: Warmes Wasser aus dem Tank wird durch die Deckenelemente geleitet und sorgt so für eine angenehme Innenraumtemperatur.

R128 ist ein nahezu vollständig rezyklierbares Gebäude. Alle baulichen Komponenten wurden als Einstoff-Bauteil ausgeführt. Die Verbindungen der einzelnen Bauteile sind leicht zugänglich und standardisiert, sodass die Montage eines Gebäudes wie R128 in ca. 10 Tagen stattfinden kann. Die Demontage und Zerlegung in einzelne sortenreine Komponenten würde sogar nur 2 bis 3 Tage in Anspruch nehmen. Beim Entwurf und bei der planerischen Durcharbeitung wurde ein besonderes Augenmerk auf die Rezyklierfähigkeit gelegt. R128 sollte beispielhaft aufzeigen, wie die (temporäre) Verwendung von Ressourcen im

The house's simple, elegant supporting structure is particularly visible at night.
Die filigrane Tragstruktur des Hauses wird bei Nacht besonders gut sichtbar.
Overleaf: The building seems to melt into the hillside and the surrounding vegetation, creating fluid boundaries between the interior and exterior spaces.
Nächste Seite: Das Gebäude scheint mit dem Hang und der Vegetation zu verschmelzen – die Grenzen zwischen Innen und Außen werden fließend.
Following page: Reflections and views through and into the building produce an impressive layering effect of various visual planes.
Übernächste Seite: Einblicke, Durchsichten und Reflexionen erzeugen eine beeindruckende Überlagerung verschiedener Bildebenen.

The complete recyclability required of R128 also meant that neither power nor communication lines, waste nor water pipes could be integrated into the ceilings or walls. As a consequence, all pipes and cables lie in covered ducts. They are thus easily accessible and can be altered or removed. The ducts run in the floor along the inside of the facades. The outlets for power, communication and water are also found in these ducts. There are no light switches in R128. Touch-free sensors and touch screens are used to control such processes as turning lights on and off, operating washbasin taps and toilet cisterns, and opening and closing windows, doors and refrigerators. The unique architectural and technological nature of R128 has lead to the building enjoying a powerful response from both specialists and the media. It resulted in a large number of documentaries being made around the world, with presenters including such famous actors as Brad Pitt. Furthermore, R128 has been used time and again as a location for television productions, including 'Tatort' and 'Soko Stuttgart' (German TV crime dramas).

Bauwesen völlig neu gedacht werden kann – ein Gedanke, der auch bei späteren Häusern immer wieder auftaucht.

Die geforderte vollständige Rezyklierbarkeit von R128 bedeutete auch, dass weder Strom- noch Kommunikationsleitungen, Wasser- oder Abwasserleitungen in Decken oder Wände integriert werden durften. Alle Leitungen liegen demnach leicht zugänglich und somit auch veränderbar bzw. entnehmbar in abgedeckten Kanälen. Diese Kanäle verlaufen im Fußboden entlang der Innenseite der Fassade. In diesen Kanälen befinden sich auch Abgabestellen für Strom, Kommunikation und Wasser. Lichtschalter gibt es in R128 nicht. Vorgänge wie das Öffnen und Schließen von Fenstern, Türen und Kühlschränken werden genauso wie das Ein- und Ausschalten der Beleuchtung oder die Betätigung der Waschtischarmaturen bzw. der Toilettenspülungen über berührungslose Sensoren bzw. über Touchscreens gesteuert. Die architektonische wie die technische Einzigartigkeit von R128 haben dazu geführt, dass das Gebäude ein intensives Echo sowohl in der Fachwelt wie auch in den Medien gefunden hat. In der Folge entstand eine Vielzahl von Dokumentarfilmen in aller Welt, unter anderem von berühmten Schauspielern wie Brad Pitt moderiert. Darüber hinaus war R128 immer wieder Spielort von Fernsehfilmen, so beispielsweise dem „Tatort" oder der „Soko Stuttgart".

H16, Tieringen
H16, Tieringen

Overleaf: The building's three-cuboid composition nestles closely into the slope.
Nächste Seite: Das aus drei Kuben komponierte Gebäude schmiegt sich eng an den Hang.

Built on a slope above a small village in the Swabian Alps, H16 was created as a continuation and extension of the concepts of ephemeral construction and the Triple Zero technologies that had been modelled for the first time in R128. H16 is less radical than R128 with regard to transparency. The reason for this is its exposed hillside location and its proximity to the village in the valley. These factors led to a much more reserved, less demonstrative design than was possible for R128.

H16 possesses a fantastic view out over a shallow, partially built-up valley. Werner Sobek was responsible for designing the building, the interior and the garden himself. As with R128, some non-local plants can be found in the immediate vicinity of the building. The further the garden leads away from the house, the more relaxed its linear layout, and the more typically indigenous the planting becomes. Stretching up to a height of over 4 m in places and moving backwards away from the house, a stepped dry stone wall made from local beige sandstone serves as a large supporting structure for the road running above the building. This retaining wall is an essential element of the overall design as it brings together the geometry, colour, and texture of the individual structures.

An einem Hang oberhalb einer kleinen Ortschaft auf der Schwäbischen Alb entstand H16 als eine Fortführung und Erweiterung der Konzepte des ephemeren Bauens und der Triple-Zero-Technologien, wie sie bei R128 erstmals exemplarisch eingesetzt worden waren. Hinsichtlich der Transparenz ist H16 weniger radikal als R128. Grund hierfür ist die exponierte Hanglage sowie die Nähe zur im Tal liegenden Ortschaft. Diese Faktoren führten zu einer sehr zurückhaltenden, weniger demonstrativen Gestaltung, als dies bei R128 der Fall sein konnte.

H16 verfügt über eine fantastische Aussicht über ein flaches, teilweise bebautes Tal. Werner Sobek zeichnete für die Gestaltung des Gebäudes selbst, ebenso für das Design der Inneneinrichtung und des Gartens verantwortlich. Wie bei R128 finden sich auch hier im unmittelbaren Bereich des Gebäudes einige ortsuntypische Pflanzen. Mit zunehmender Entfernung vom Haus lockert die Linienführung des Gartens zunehmend auf, wird die Bepflanzung zunehmend ortstypisch. Eine bereichsweise mehr als 4 m hohe, nach hinten abgestufte Trockenmauer aus beigefarbigem lokalem Sandstein dient als große Stützmauer zu der oberhalb des Gebäudes verlaufenden Straße. Diese Stützmauer ist ein wesentliches Element des Gesamtentwurfs, da sie die einzelnen Baukörper in ihrer Geometrie, Farbigkeit und Textur zusammenhält.

From a compositional point of view, H16 is a three-body problem. When designing this widely visible house on a slope, careful compositional studies were carried out to determine the volume, colour, surfaces, and position of the three cuboid structures as they relate to one another. One of the cuboids contains the bedrooms, bathrooms, children's rooms, and utility rooms. The clients wished to have a private area in this space, so the structure was surrounded with black-dyed precast concrete panels that are only interrupted by a few windows in the form of vertical strips. Viewed from afar, the cuboid appears enclosed. Narrow, vertical strips of window reminiscent of a barcode provide views outwards and ensure a generous supply of daylight – without leaving too much of the interior visible from the world outside. A totally transparent second cuboid containing a kitchen, an eating space, and a living area is placed on top of the first black construction. The upper cuboid lies slightly offset above the one below, creating covered zones in front of the lower structure that provide favourite outdoor areas for use in summer. A third cuboid stands slightly apart from the others. Made from grey concrete, it functions as a garage, a technical centre, and a space for hobbies and storage. This grey cuboid is connected with the two others via a large, terrace-shaped platform. Great care was taken over the proportioning of the building's

Kompositorisch gesehen handelt es sich bei H16 um ein Drei-Quader-Problem. Volumen, Farbigkeit, Oberflächen und Positionierung der Quader zueinander sind das Ergebnis sorgfältiger Kompositionsstudien für dieses von Weitem sichtbare Haus am Hang. Einer der Quader enthält Schlafzimmer, Bäder, Kinderzimmer und Hauswirtschaftsräume. Aufgrund der von der Bauherrschaft gewünschten Privatsphäre in diesem Bereich wurde der Quader mit schwarz eingefärbten Betonfertigteilen umgeben, die nur von wenigen Fensterflächen in Form vertikal angeordneter Streifen unterbrochen werden. Der Block wirkt, von Weitem gesehen, geschlossen. Schmale vertikale Fensterstreifen, die an einen Barcode erinnern, erlauben Ausblicke und sorgen für großzügige Versorgung mit Tageslicht – ohne jedoch den Blick ins Innere zu weit zu öffnen. Aufgesetzt auf den schwarzen Quader befindet sich ein vollkommen transparenter zweiter Quader, der Küche, Ess- und Wohnbereich beinhaltet. Der obere Quader ruht leicht versetzt auf dem unteren, sodass vor dem unteren Quader überdeckte Zonen entstehen, die im Sommer gern benutzte Außenflächen darstellen. Ein dritter Quader steht ein wenig abseits. Er ist in grauem Beton gehalten und beinhaltet die Funktionen Garage, Technikzentrale und Vorrats- sowie Hobbyräume. Der graue Quader ist durch eine große, terrassenförmige Plattform mit den beiden

The position of the house, which lies embedded in the topography of the slope, is underlined by the dry stone wall made from natural stone.

Eine Trockenmauer aus Naturstein unterstreicht die Einbettung des Hauses in die Topografie des Hangs.

Overleaf: The upper storey's transparent cuboid contains a cooking, living and eating area.

Nächste Seite: Der transparente Kubus im Obergeschoss umfasst Küche, Wohn- und Essbereich.

Layout of the ground floor.
Grundriss des Erdgeschosses.
The transition between shaded and sunlit areas also provides a high level of user comfort in the exterior space.
Der Wechsel zwischen verschatteten und sonnenbeschienenen Bereichen sorgt auch im Außenbereich für hohen Nutzerkomfort.

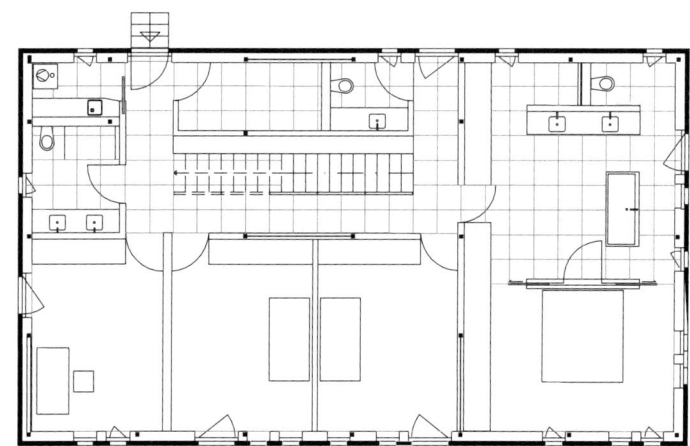

The bathroom is located in the lower cuboid – vertical strips of window allow a great deal of daylight into the building whilst also providing a good level of privacy.

Das Badezimmer liegt im unteren Kubus – vertikale Fensterstreifen lassen viel Tageslicht ins Innere, sorgen aber auch für guten Blickschutz.

The living and dining area offers a sweeping view of the valley – the natural modulation of colours and light becomes an intrinsic part of the day-to-day experience.

Der Wohn- und Essbereich bietet einen weiten Blick ins Tal – der natürliche Wechsel von Farben und Helligkeit wird zum selbstverständlichen Bestandteil des täglichen Erlebens.

structures, resulting in a formally balanced ensemble. This high formal equilibrium is further underlined by the choice of surfaces and colours for the cuboids themselves.

With H16, a great deal of importance was placed on varying the tactile qualities of the structures' surfaces. For this reason, the black-coloured precast concrete panels on the lower cuboid were hewn by hand, resulting in a deeply textured exterior with a surface roughness depth of up to 10 mm. The surfaces of the technical cuboid, which is also made of concrete, were stained with acid to create a finely pored, slightly raw exterior. The two cuboids are connected with large, natural stone slabs taken from local quarries. In its minimalism and transparency, the raised glass cuboid presents a totally smooth shell that contrasts with that of the structures below. All of the handrails were made using glass-bead blasted stainless steel tubes – a material which allows one's hand to glide effortlessly across its surface. In terms of its energy concept, H16 is a low-energy house. The roof area of the glazed cuboid is covered with flat photovoltaic elements. Geothermal energy is used to provide heat for the building.

anderen Quadern verbunden. Durch die sorgfältige Proportionierung der Baukörper entsteht ein formal ausgeglichenes Ensemble. Diese hohe formale Ausgewogenheit wird durch die Wahl der Farbigkeiten der Quader und ihrer Oberflächen weiter unterstrichen.

Bei H16 wurde sehr viel Wert auf eine Variation der taktilen Qualitäten der Bauteiloberflächen gelegt. So wurden die schwarz gefärbten Betonfertigteile des unteren Quaders von Hand behauen, bis eine tiefenstrukturierte Oberfläche mit bis zu 10 mm Rautiefe entstand. Der ebenfalls aus Beton bestehende Technikquader wurde an den Oberflächen angesäuert, sodass eine feinporige, leicht raue Oberfläche entstand. Beide Quader werden durch große, aus heimischen Steinbrüchen gewonnenen Natursteinplatten miteinander verbunden. Der aufgesetzte gläserne Quader bietet in seiner Minimalität und Transparenz vollkommen glatte, zu den unteren Quadern kontrastierende Oberflächen. Alle Handläufe wurden aus mit Glasperlen gestrahlten Edelstahlrohren hergestellt. Auf diesen Handläufen kann eine Hand tatsächlich „laufen". Vom Energiekonzept her stellt H16 ein Niedrigenergiehaus dar. Die Dachfläche des gläsernen Quaders ist mit flachen Fotovoltaik-Elementen belegt. Die Heizenergie wird durch Geothermie gewonnen.

S3, Southern Germany
S3, Süddeutschland

S3 lies on the edge of a small town around one hour's drive north of Stuttgart. The building site consists of four combined plots of land at the end of a cul-de-sac. Following on from R128 and H16, the house represents yet more meticulous compositional work. Embedded in a patchwork landscape of small plots, particular care was needed when dividing up S3's comparatively large living space into separate areas. A cuboid clad in black cement panels with vertical strips of window reminiscent of a barcode (similar to H16) contains the house's sleeping and sanitary rooms. The glazed entrance hall, which also provides access to the upper floor, stands perpendicular to this structure. Like the entrance hall itself, the upper storey also consists of a fully glazed cuboid. This area is designed for living, working and cooking. The glass cuboid grants access to the garden and a large outdoor swimming pool located on the same level.

S3 liegt am Rande einer Kleinstadt, ca. eine Autostunde nördlich von Stuttgart. Vier zusammengelegte Grundstücke, am Ende einer Sackgasse gelegen, bilden das Baugrundstück. In der Nachfolge von R128 und H16 stellt das Gebäude S3 erneut eine sehr sorgfältige kompositorische Arbeit dar. Eingebettet in eine kleinteilige Umgebung war die vergleichsweise große Wohnfläche von S3 besonders sorgfältig auf einzelne Gebäudebereiche zu verteilen. Ein mit schwarzen Zementplatten verkleideter Quader, dessen vertikale Fensterbänder (ähnlich wie bei H16) an einen Barcode erinnern, bildet die Umhüllung für die Schlaf- und Sanitärräume des Hauses. Senkrecht zu diesem Quader steht die verglaste Eingangshalle, über die man auch in das Obergeschoss gelangt. Das Obergeschoss besteht ebenso wie die Eingangshalle aus einem vollkommen verglasten Quader. Dieser Bereich ist für Wohnen, Arbeiten und Kochen vorgesehen. Vom Glasquader aus gelangt man ebenerdig in den Garten und zu einem großen Außenschwimmbecken.

Overleaf: S3 is also distinguished by its careful integration into the landscape.
Nächste Seite: Auch S3 zeichnet sich durch seine sorgsame Einbettung in die Landschaft aus.

S3's three-body composition is integrated harmoniously into the gentle slope. The garages and the technical rooms are covered in earth. The ground plan of the building's three cuboid structures and the outdoor swimming pool form a U shape that encloses a garden. Laid out with great care, this garden boasts a number of magnificent trees that provide an important optical counterweight to the building. Heating and warm water for the house are provided using a heat pump and a connected geothermal probe. The roof area of the glazed cuboid is covered in photovoltaic panels that generate the electrical energy required for the systems technology. The outdoor swimming pool is fitted with an integrated solar collector and is thus heated in a natural manner.

The building envelope is highly insulated. All of the transparent spaces are fitted with triple-pane insulated glazing that is supplemented with an internal sun shield. This solar protection is coated in vaporised silver and thus contributes to UV reflection. A building automation system ensures maximal user comfort and an optimal interior climate.

Die Drei-Quader-Komposition von S3 fügt sich harmonisch in den leicht geneigten Hang ein. Die Garagen und die Technikräume sind erdüberdeckt. Die Baukörper und das Außenschwimmbecken bilden im Grundriss eine U-Form, die einen Garten umschließt. Dieser mit großer Sorgfalt angelegte Garten verfügt über eine Reihe prächtiger Bäume, die ein wichtiges optisches Gegengewicht zum Gebäude bilden. Das Gebäude wird mithilfe einer Wärmepumpe und daran gekoppelte Erdwärmesonden beheizt bzw. mit Warmwasser versorgt. Die mit Fotovoltaik-Paneelen belegte Dachfläche des verglasten Quaders liefert die für die Anlagentechnik erforderliche elektrische Energie. Der außen liegende Swimmingpool besitzt einen integrierten Sonnenkollektor und wird so auf natürliche Weise aufgewärmt.

Die Gebäudehülle ist hoch gedämmt. In den transparenten Bereichen wurde eine Dreischeiben-Isolierverglasung eingesetzt, die durch einen innen liegenden Sonnenschutz ergänzt wird. Dieser Sonnenschutz ist silberbedampft und trägt so zur UV-Reflexion bei. Eine Gebäudeautomation sorgt für maximalen Nutzerkomfort und optimales Raumklima.

As well as a large garden, the exterior space includes a swimming pool heated by a solar collector.
Der Außenbereich umfasst neben einem großen Garten auch ein durch einen Sonnenkollektor erwärmtes Schwimmbecken.
Overleaf: The living area opens onto the garden, creating fluid transitions between the interior and exterior spaces.
Nächste Seite: Der Wohnbereich öffnet sich zum Garten – die Übergänge zwischen Innen und Außen werden fließend.

Site plan, elevation and floor plans.
Lageplan, Ansicht und Grundrisse.
Overleaf: The cuboids seem to hover over the ground – the architecture takes its cue from the landscape without disrupting it.
Nächste Seite: Die Kuben scheinen über dem Boden zu schweben – die Architektur orientiert sich an der Landschaft, verletzt sie aber nicht.

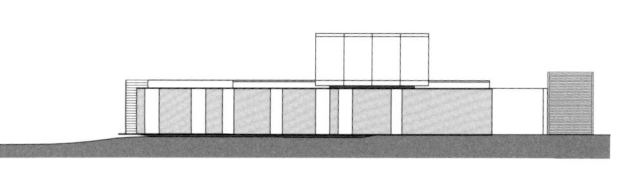

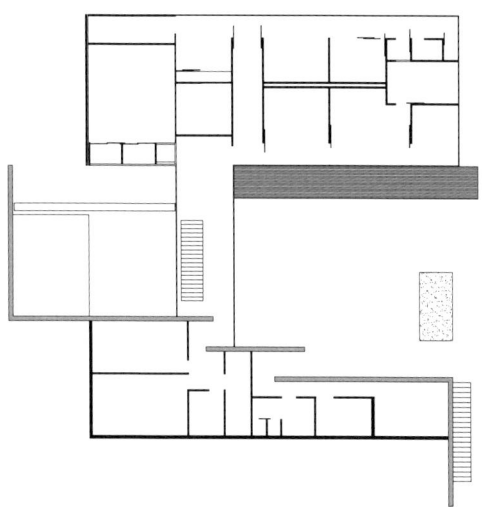
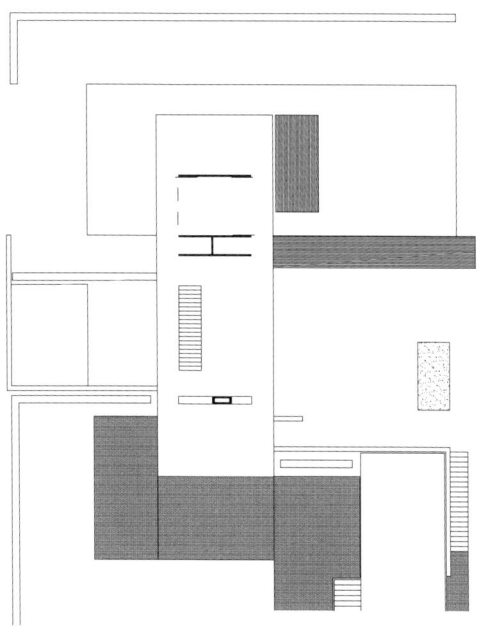

D10, Biberach

D10, a single-family house located to the south of Ulm, heralded in the era of Plus-Energy houses designed by Werner Sobek. On their backland building plot with its old stock of trees, the clients wished to create a home for two people that would be groundbreaking with regard to technology, living comfort and aesthetics. They also wanted the house to feature a maximum of transparency. In addition, it was also desired that the concepts of fluid space and the connection between the interior and the exterior spaces be interpreted afresh and further developed. The architectural answer to the clients' wishes is a clearly structured, single-storey bungalow with a cellar and a garage. The bungalow consists of two parallel rendered walls and an exterior facade. The latter is made of glazing that reaches from the floor to the ceiling. The exterior appearance is defined by the extensively protruding white floor slab and the flat roof, the white outer edge of which tops off the ensemble. The roof sits on the walls and a few slim steel supports. This makes it appear weightless and floating, allowing the interior and exterior spaces to merge into an optical whole.

The look of the house is determined by a series of meticulously designed details. Part of the floor slab hovers above the ground so that the greenery of the garden can reach right under the edge of the

Das südlich von Ulm befindliche Einfamilienhaus D10 stellt den Eintritt in die Ära der von Werner Sobek geplanten Plusenergiehäuser dar. Wunsch der Bauherren war es, auf ihrem in der zweiten Reihe befindlichen Grundstück mit altem Baumbestand ein in Bezug auf Technologie, Wohnkomfort und Ästhetik zukunftweisendes Wohnhaus für zwei Personen zu errichten. Das Haus sollte maximale Transparenz aufweisen. Die Ideen des fließenden Raumes und der Verbindung von Innenraum und Außenbereich sollte neu interpretiert und weiterentwickelt werden. Die architektonische Antwort auf die Wünsche der Bauherren ist ein klar gegliederter, eingeschossiger Bungalow mit Kellergeschoss und Garage. Der Bungalow besteht aus zwei parallel gestellten verputzten Wänden und einer Außenfassade. Letztere besteht aus einer vom Boden zur Decke reichenden Verglasung. Das äußere Erscheinungsbild wird durch die weit auskragende weiße Bodenplatte und durch das mit einer weißen Außenkante abschließende Flachdach bestimmt. Das Dach ruht auf den Wandscheiben und wenigen schlanken Stahlstützen. Dadurch wirkt es schwerelos und scheint zu schweben. Innen- und Außenbereich können so zu einer optischen Einheit verschmelzen.

Die Erscheinungsform des Gebäudes wird durch eine Reihe sehr behutsam geplanter Details bestimmt. Die Bodenplatte schwebt zum Teil

Overleaf: The shade cast by the extensively projecting wooden roof also provides thermal comfort on hot summer days.

Nächste Seite: Die Verschattung durch das weit auskragende Holzdach sorgt auch an heißen Sommertagen für thermischen Komfort.

building. The same white floor slab runs from the interior to the exterior of the house, thus simultaneously serving both as a terrace (outside) and the floor (inside) – of course, in spite of this optical continuum, the spaces are thermally separated. The two parallel sections of wall are also located both in the interior and the exterior of the building. The constituent elements of the interior space thus simultaneously function as the constituent elements of the exterior space. The storey-high glazing with its barely visible mullions assists with this impression of continuity. Further details also support this artistic goal: for instance, the photovoltaic system on the flat roof has only been set at a slight gradient and is placed far back from the structure's forward edge. This renders it barely visible from the garden.

The bungalow's basement and floor slab are made of concrete. For reasons of complete recyclability, no kind of external sealant has been used on the concrete structure. It is therefore neither tanked (coated with bitumen, etc.), nor does it have any integral waterproofing properties. Instead, the entire concrete body has been laid on foam glass plates. Large areas of wall were filled with recycled concrete material. This disperses any surface water that seeps in, causing it flow away from the concrete structure itself. The development of this ideal, recycling-friendly

über dem Erdreich, sodass das Grün des Gartens bis unter die Gebäudekante greifen kann. Die weiße Bodenplatte läuft von innen nach außen, ist somit gleichermaßen (im Außenbereich) Terrasse wie (im Innenraum) Fußboden – trotz der optischen Kontinuität ist sie aber natürlich thermisch getrennt. Die beiden parallel gestellten Wandscheiben befinden sich ebenfalls sowohl im Innen- als auch im Außenraum. Die konstituierenden Elemente des Innenbereichs sind gleichzeitig auch die konstituierenden Elemente des Außenbereichs. Die geschosshohe Verglasung mit ihren optisch kaum in Erscheinung tretenden Pfosten unterstützt diesen Ausdruck von Kontinuität. Weitere Details unterstützen die gestalterische Intention: So wurde die Fotovoltaik-Anlage auf dem Flachdach nur mit geringer Neigung und zudem von der vorderen Dachkante weit zurückgesetzt verlegt. Auf diese Weise ist sie vom Garten aus kaum erkennbar.

Das Untergeschoss und die Bodenplatte des Bungalows bestehen aus Beton. Aus Gründen der vollständigen Rezyklierbarkeit wurde auf jedwede äußere Abdichtung des Betonkörpers verzichtet. Er stellt somit weder eine schwarze noch eine weiße Wanne dar. Der gesamte Betonkörper wurde vielmehr auf Schaumglasplatten aufgesetzt. Die Wände wurden großräumig mit einer Schüttung aus Recyclingbeton angefüllt. Einsickerndes Oberflächenwasser wird auf diese Weise entspannt und

The fluid transition between the interior and exterior spaces is underlined by the continuity of the floor and ceiling surfaces.
Der fließende Übergang zwischen Innen und Außen wird durch die Kontinuität der Beläge von Boden und Decke unterstrichen.
Overleaf: The bathroom and bedroom are shielded from view in the area behind the library.
Nächste Seite: Bad und Schlafzimmer befinden sich im blickgeschützten Bereich hinter der Bibliothek.

solution was able to take place thanks to the position of the groundwater below the basement footing. The walls and the roof of the bungalow consist of a highly insulated timber construction. As it has been created with as few adhesive bonds and composite structures as possible, the building is as recyclable as it can be. Easily detachable joints have been used wherever feasible.

A ventilation and extraction system with highly efficient heat recovery capabilities reliably provides all areas with fresh air. When required, a quick manual change of air is possible via the large sliding doors. A uniform interior temperature is achieved throughout the year with the help of vertical geothermal probes, a heat pump, and underfloor heating and cooling. Despite its compact nature and the fully glazed facades to the east, south and west, D10 achieves a surplus of energy in terms of its annual results. The building's excellent energy performance is achieved by the minimisation of energy consumption and the maximisation of energy generation. The major contribution to minimising energy consumption is made by the high level of thermal insulation and the efficient systems technology. Energy production is maximised via the photovoltaic system, geothermal energy and the windows (thanks to solar heat gains). The photovoltaic modules produce more than 7,500 kWh per annum.

fließt vom Betonkörper entfernt ab. Da der Grundwasserspiegel unterhalb der Kellersohle ansteht, konnte auf diese Weise eine recyclingtechnisch vorbildliche Lösung entwickelt werden. Die Wände und das Dach des Bungalows bestehen aus einer hoch wärmegedämmten Holzkonstruktion. Das Gebäude ist weitestgehend rezyklierbar, da so weit wie möglich ohne Klebeverbindungen und Verbundkonstruktionen realisiert. Wo immer möglich wurden einfach lösbare Verbindungen eingesetzt.

Eine Be- und Entlüftungsanlage mit hocheffizienter Wärmerückgewinnung versorgt alle Bereiche zuverlässig mit Frischluft. Durch die großformatigen Schiebetüren ist bei Bedarf ein sehr schneller manueller Luftwechsel möglich. Eine gleichbleibende Temperatur im Innenraum wird mithilfe von vertikalen Erdsonden, Wärmepumpe und Fußboden-Heizung bzw. -Kühlung ganzjährig erreicht. D10 erreicht trotz seiner Kompaktheit und der voll verglasten Fassaden an der Ost-, Süd- und Westseite in der Jahresbilanz einen Überschuss an Energie. Das exzellente energetische Verhalten des Gebäudes wird durch eine Minimierung des Verbrauchs und durch die Maximierung der Energiegewinne erreicht. Zur Minimierung tragen v. a. gute Wärmedämmung und die effiziente Anlagentechnik bei. Die Maximierung wird über die Fotovoltaik-Anlage, die Geothermie und (dank der solaren Gewinne) die Fenster erreicht. Die

The position and orientation of the house were carefully adapted around the site's magnificent stock of trees.

Lage und Ausrichtung des Hauses wurden sorgfältig an den wunderschönen Baumbestand des Grundstücks angepasst.

Overleaf: The roof sits on two sections of wall and a few steel supports – an important feature that permits the lightness and openness of the interior space.

Nächste Seite: Das Dach ruht auf zwei Wandscheiben und wenigen Stahlstützen – wichtige Voraussetzung für Leichtigkeit und Offenheit des Innenraums.

As with Werner Sobek's other houses, D10 sits on the ground without causing it any harm.

Wie die anderen Häuser von Werner Sobek ruht auch D10 auf dem Boden, ohne ihn zu verletzen.

The geothermal probes cool and heat the building as required via a concrete core temperature control system, which predominantly delivers its energy in an upward direction. Over the course of the year, the geothermal probes deposit and withdraw heat from the ground, which thus serves as a large seasonal heat store. The passive solar gains captured through the windows are another important factor: 66% of the total heating requirement is covered in this way. The south-facing glazing even exhibits a positive energy balance thanks to its very good g-values (incident solar radiation values) and U-values (thermal transmittance coefficients). At the time of year when heating is required, the facade captures more solar energy from the low-lying sun than it loses to the world outside. Even when the sky is overcast, the diffuse light still permits solar gains. This heats the building every day, meaning that the heat pump and the underfloor heating only see occasional use.

Fotovoltaik produziert mehr als 7.500 kWh/a. Die Erdsonden kühlen bzw. heizen das Gebäude je nach Bedarf über eine Betonkerntemperierung, die ihre Energie vor allem nach oben abgibt. Das Erdreich wird über die Erdsonden im Jahresrhythmus be- und entladen und dient somit als großer saisonaler Wärmespeicher. Ein weiterer wichtiger Aspekt sind die passiven solaren Gewinne durch die Fenster. Immerhin 66% des gesamten Heizwärmebedarfs werden auf diese Weise gedeckt. Die Südverglasung weist durch die sehr guten g- (Energiedurchlassgrade) und U-Werte (Wärmedurchgangskoeffizienten) sogar eine positive Energiebilanz auf. Während der Heizperiode fängt sie durch die tief stehende Sonne mehr Solarenergie ein, als sie nach außen verliert. Selbst bei bedecktem Himmel ermöglicht die diffuse Strahlung noch solare Gewinne. Dadurch wird das Gebäude täglich aufgeladen und muss nur gelegentlich auf Wärmepumpe und Fußbodenheizung zurückgreifen.

Elevation, ground floor layout, basement layout.
Ansicht, Grundriss des Erdgeschosses, Grundriss des Untergeschosses.
Overleaf: A sliding wall element embellished with gold leaf allows the kitchen area to be fully or partially closed off.
Nächste Seite: Ein mit Blattgold verziertes, verschiebbares Wandelement ermöglicht ein partielles oder völliges Abschließen des Küchenbereichs.

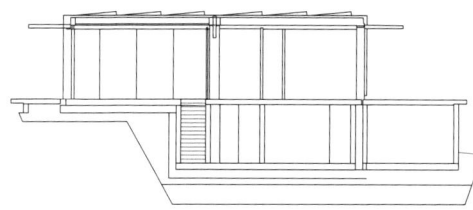

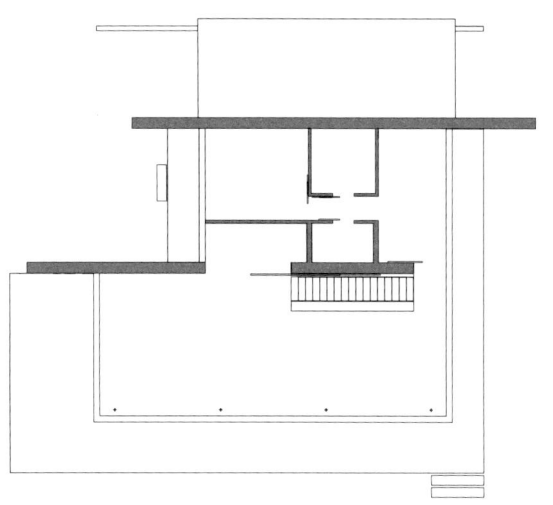 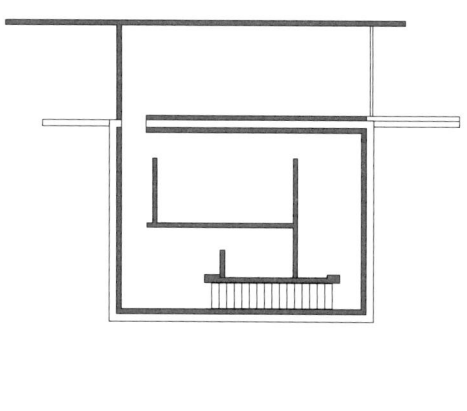

F87, Berlin

F87 (given the project name 'Efficiency House Plus with Electromobility' by the supporting Federal Ministry) was the result of an architectural planning competition initiated by the former Ministry for Transport, Building and Urban Development in 2010. The goal of the competition was to demonstrate 'the current developmental state of the networking of energy-efficient, sustainable construction and living by means of a fully built, architecturally attractive research project.' After the competition was decided in Werner Sobek's favour at the start of 2011, the entire planning and execution had to be completed in the space of a few months to allow the project to be opened by the German Chancellor in early December, 2011.

F87 is situated in a central location in inner city Berlin. The two-storey house includes a section that is not overlooked from the street. This unit faces a peaceful green space and contains a residence for four people. The part of the building facing the street consists of a two-storey glass facade framed in a portal-like structure. This area is freely accessible and allows visitors – who are protected from the elements – to learn about the building and its energy performance from flat screens on the portal's interior walls. The glass front also offers a view of the 'energy core' located immediately behind the facade on the ground floor.

F87 (offizieller Projektname des fördernden Bundesministeriums: „Effizienzhaus Plus mit Elektromobilität") ging aus einem Realisierungswettbewerb hervor, den das damalige Bundesministerium für Verkehr, Bau und Stadtentwicklung 2010 ausgelobt hatte. Ziel des Wettbewerbs war es, „anhand eines real gebauten, architektonisch attraktiven Forschungs-Pilotprojektes den Stand der Entwicklung in der Vernetzung von energieeffizientem, nachhaltigen Bauen und Wohnen" aufzuzeigen. Nachdem der Wettbewerb Anfang 2011 zugunsten von Werner Sobek entschieden wurde, musste innerhalb weniger Monate die gesamte Planung und Ausführung erfolgen, um eine Eröffnung des Projekts durch die Bundeskanzlerin Anfang Dezember 2011 zu ermöglichen.

F87 liegt in zentraler Lage in der Berliner Innenstadt. Das zweigeschossige Haus besitzt einen von der Straße nicht einsehbaren Gartenteil. Dieser Gartenteil ist einer ruhigen Grünfläche zugewandt und beinhaltet eine Wohnung für vier Personen. Der Straßenseite zugewandt ist eine portalartig eingerahmte zweigeschossige Glasfassade. Dieser Bereich ist frei zugänglich und erlaubt Besuchern, sich – geschützt vor der Witterung – an Flachbildschirmen an den Innenseiten des Portals über das Gebäude und seine energetische „Performance" zu informieren. Darüber hinaus bietet die Glasfassade einen Einblick in den „Energiekern", der sich unmittelbar hinter der Fassade im Erdgeschoss befindet.

Overleaf: The covered entrance area offers a good view of the building's technical core.
Nächste Seite: Der überdachte Eingangsbereich bietet einen guten Blick auf den Technikern des Gebäudes.

Oblique section views showing the close interlinkage of electromobility, the technical core, and the living space.
Die Schrägschnitte zeigen die enge Verknüpfung von Elektromobilität, Technikkern und Wohnbereich.
Overleaf: The house's living quarters face away from the street, affording a combination of transparency and privacy.
Nächste Seite: Der Wohnbereich des Hauses ist von der Straße abgewandt und ermöglicht so die Verbindung von Transparenz und Privatheit.

Originally intended to be used for three years, F87's tenancy was extended by another three years in the face of enormous visitor interest. Apart from its short service life and its prominent urban location, various other specifications had to be taken into account. Naturally, the building had to be designed and built to achieve full recyclability. The greatest possible level of user comfort also had to be guaranteed for the two 'test families' who would each live in the building for one year. In addition, the structure had to be suitable for use as an information centre before, between and after the residential periods. Moreover, the building had to be a zero-emission house that would generate enough energy to completely power itself, an electric bicycle and two electric cars.

The building uses all the available construction space, thus maximising the roof area which can be employed to generate energy via photovoltaics. The closed facade on the north side minimises thermal losses. The south facade, which is equipped with photovoltaics, maximises the amount of energy generated. The entrance to the house is found on the west side where the electric cars are also parked and charged. The residential spaces are shared over two levels: the living and dining areas are found on the ground floor, and the bedrooms are located on the upper storey. The 'energy core', which houses all of the building's

Ursprünglich nur für eine Nutzungsdauer von drei Jahren vorgesehen, wurde die Nutzung von F87 angesichts des enormen Besucherinteresses um weitere drei Jahre verlängert. Neben der kurzen Standzeit und der exponierten städtebaulichen Lage waren noch diverse andere Anforderungen zu berücksichtigen. Das Gebäude sollte natürlich so geplant und gebaut werden, dass es vollkommen rezyklierbar ist. Größtmöglicher Nutzerkomfort für zwei jeweils 1 Jahr im Gebäude wohnende „Testfamilien" musste genauso sichergestellt werden wie die Verwendbarkeit als Informationszentrum vor, zwischen und nach der Wohnnutzung. Darüber hinaus musste das Gebäude ein Nullemissionshaus sein und zudem so viel Energie erzeugen, dass es sich selbst sowie die beiden zum Gebäude gehörenden Elektrofahrzeuge und ein Elektrofahrrad vollständig mit Energie versorgen kann.

Das Gebäude nutzt das gesamte zur Verfügung gestellte Baufeld und maximiert dadurch die Dachfläche, die zur Energiegewinnung durch Fotovoltaik verwendet werden kann. Die geschlossene Fassade auf der Nordseite minimiert die thermischen Verluste. Die mit Fotovoltaik belegte Südfassade maximiert den Energiegewinn. Der Zugang zum Haus erfolgt auf der Westseite, wo auch die Elektrofahrzeuge geparkt und geladen werden. Die Wohnräume verteilen sich auf zwei Ebenen:

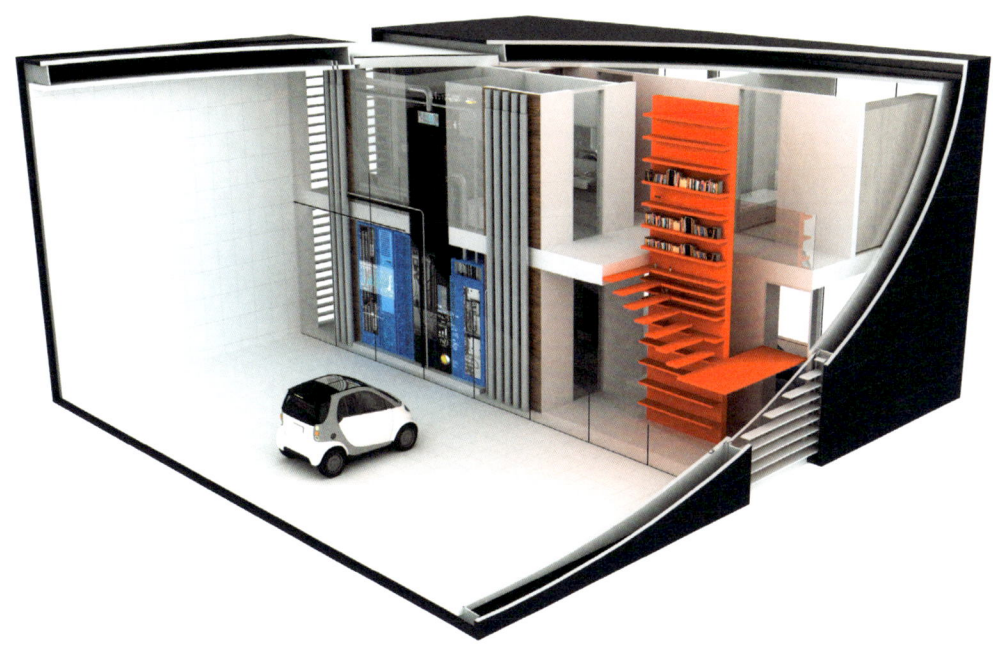

technical functions, is a visible representation of the interface between electromobility and the property. The energy concept unites both tried-and-tested and innovative components. Energy is generated from two sources. The use of geothermal energy was avoided as the expense for removing the geothermal probes would have been disproportionately high in view of their limited service life. Instead, an air-to-water heat pump is used to extract the energy for heating and warm water production from the air outside. Photovoltaic panels on the roof and on the south facade generate electricity. Power produced in this manner can be consumed straight away, employed later on (after being temporarily stored in the house's own 40 kWh lithium-ion battery) or used to charge the electric vehicles. Any additional electricity can be fed into the public mains. Innovative technology and intelligent energy management allow the battery to function bidirectionally – that is, both as a consumer and a supplier of energy for both the house and the public grid.

On average, F87 produces more than 16,000 kWh per annum. The building itself requires approx. 10,000 kWh per annum for all its functions. The substantial energy surplus is used to power the electric vehicles. These have a total requirement of around 6,000 kWh per annum (with an assumed combined mileage of approx. 25,000 km per annum for both cars and around 4,000 km per annum for the electric

Im Erdgeschoss liegt der Wohn- und Essbereich, die Schlafzimmer liegen im Obergeschoss. Der „Energiekern", der alle technischen Funktionen des Hauses beherbergt, stellt die Schnittstelle zwischen Immobilie und Elektromobilität anschaulich dar. Das Energiekonzept vereint bewährte und innovative Komponenten. Energie wird aus zwei Quellen gewonnen. Auf die Nutzung von Geothermie wurde verzichtet, da der Aufwand für den Rückbau der Erdsonden angesichts der begrenzten Standdauer unverhältnismäßig hoch gewesen wäre. Stattdessen kommt eine Luft-Wasser-Wärmepumpe zum Einsatz, die die Energie zum Heizen und zur Warmwasserbereitung aus der Außenluft gewinnt. Fotovoltaik-Paneele auf dem Dach und an der Südfassade erzeugen Strom. Der so erzeugte Strom kann sofort oder – nach einer Zwischenspeicherung in der hausinternen 40-kWh-Lithium-Ionen-Batterie – zu einem späteren Zeitpunkt verbraucht bzw. zum Laden der Elektrofahrzeuge verwendet werden. Darüber hinaus anfallender Strom kann in das öffentliche Versorgungsnetz eingespeist werden. Durch innovative Technologie und intelligentes Energiemanagement kann die Batterie bidirektional, d. h. sowohl als Energieabnehmer als auch als Energielieferant dienen – für das Haus ebenso wie für das öffentliche Netz.

Screens in the entrance area provide interested visitors with information about the building's sustainability performance. Bildschirme im Eingangsbereich bieten interessierten Besuchern Informationen über die Nachhaltigkeitsperformance des Gebäudes.
Overleaf: The charging station for the electric vehicles is located right in front of the house. Nächste Seite: Die Ladestation für die Elektrofahrzeuge befindet sich direkt vor dem Haus.

Layout of the ground floor and the upper storey.
Grundriss Erdgeschoss und Obergeschoss.

bicycle). The photovoltaic modules on the roof and on the south facade thus generate enough energy per year on average to cover the total requirements of both the house and the electric vehicles – 'my house, my fuelling station'.

A mechanical ventilation and extraction system provides a high quality of air in the interior space. Each inhabited room in the house can also be ventilated manually. The heat contained in the extracted air is recovered before the exhaust air is fed into the gap between the earth and the elevated floor panel. Bundling the building technology together within the energy core means that all service lines can be kept short. All distribution and ventilation ducts are as short as possible and thermally insulated, allowing distribution losses to be reduced to an absolute minimum. The building's inhabitants can consult and control all of the household technology and the charging equipment using two touch panels in the house and via smartphones.

The house sits on a shallow foundation of removable, precast concrete elements. The house itself was built using a timber panel construction. Single steel supports along the totally glazed east and west facades help bear the load of the ceiling and roof construction. Cellulose fibre insulation was blown into the cavities in the walls and ceilings.

F87 produziert im Durchschnitt mehr als 16.000 kWh/a. Das Gebäude selbst benötigt für alle seine Funktionen ca. 10.000 kWh/a. Mit dem beachtlichen Energieüberschuss werden die Elektrofahrzeuge versorgt. Diese haben (bei einer angenommenen Fahrleistung der beiden Autos von insgesamt ca. 25.000 km/a und des Elektrofahrrads von ca. 4.000 km/a) einen Bedarf von insgesamt ca. 6.000 kWh/a. Die Fotovoltaik-Module auf dem Dach und an der Südfassade erzeugen somit im Jahresmittel ausreichend Energie, um den kompletten Bedarf des Hauses und der Elektrofahrzeuge zu decken – „Mein Haus, meine Tankstelle".

Eine mechanische Be- und Entlüftung sorgt für eine sehr gute Innenraumluftqualität. Jeder bewohnte Raum des Hauses kann zusätzlich manuell belüftet werden. Die in der Abluft enthaltene Wärme wird zurückgewonnen, bevor die Abluft in den Zwischenraum zwischen Erdreich und aufgeständerter Bodenplatte eingeleitet wird. Durch die Bündelung der Gebäudetechnik im Energiekern können die Leitungswege kurz gehalten werden. Alle Verteiler und Luftkanäle sind so kurz wie möglich; darüber hinaus sind sie auch wärmegedämmt – Verteilverluste können somit auf ein absolutes Minimum reduziert werden. Die Bewohner des Gebäudes können die gesamte Haustechnik ebenso wie die Ladetechnik über zwei Touchpanels im Haus sowie über Smartphones einsehen und steuern.

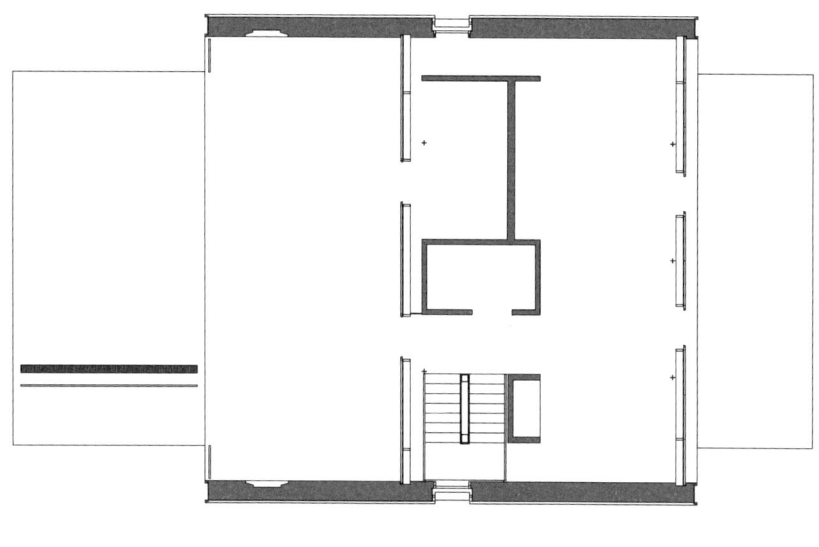
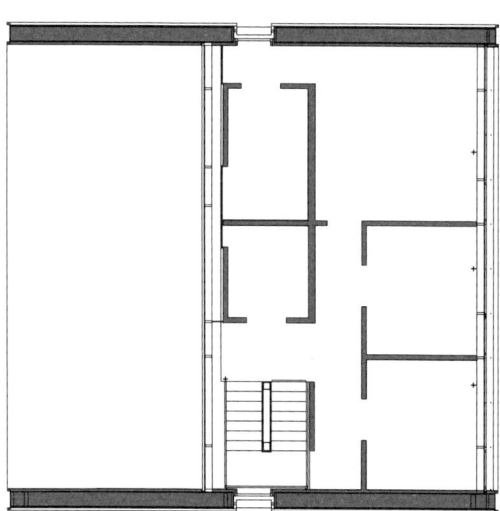

This provides a very good insulating effect. Additional hemp insulation ensures a high level of acoustic comfort in the interior space. All of the floor and wall coverings were installed without adhesives. This allows the easily identifiable materials to be sorted into homogeneous groups as simply and as comprehensively as possible during the conversion or dismantling process.

The large glass facades are equipped with triple-insulated glazing; the space between the panes is filled with noble gas (argon). Furthermore, the glass facade on the east side of the building has an external sun shield made from aluminium slats that can be controlled both automatically and manually. The closed facades are fitted with back-ventilated thin-film photovoltaic modules on the south side. Optically equivalent, colour printed glass was deployed on the north side; although these glass panels do not generate electricity, they do ensure a unified appearance. The roof surface is almost completely covered in monocrystalline photovoltaic modules.

Das Haus ruht auf einer Flachgründung aus wieder entnehmbaren Betonfertigteilen. Das Gebäude selbst wurde in Holztafelbauweise ausgeführt. Entlang der vollständig verglasten Ost- und Westfassade dienen einzelne Stahlstützen als zusätzliche Auflager für die Decken- und Dachkonstruktion. Zwischen die Gefache der Wände und Decken wird Zellulose eingeblasen. Dies sorgt für eine sehr gute Dämmwirkung. Eine zusätzliche Hanfdämmung sorgt für hohen akustischen Komfort im Innenraum. Sämtliche Boden- und Wandbeläge werden ohne Verklebung angebracht, um bei einem Um- oder Rückbau eine einfache und möglichst sortenreine Trennung klar identifizierbarer Materialen zu erlauben.

Die großen Glasfassaden sind mit Dreifach-Isolierverglasung versehen; der Scheibenzwischenraum ist mit Argon (Edelgas) gefüllt. Die Glasfassade auf der Ostseite des Gebäudes besitzt darüber hinaus einen außen liegenden Sonnenschutz aus Aluminium-Lamellen, der sowohl automatisch als auch manuell gesteuert werden kann. Die geschlossenen Fassaden sind südseitig mit hinterlüfteten Dünnschicht-Fotovoltaik-Modulen versehen. An der Nordseite wurden optisch gleichwertige, farbig bedruckte Gläser eingesetzt; diese Gläser erzeugen keinen Strom, sorgen aber für ein einheitliches Erscheinungsbild. Die Dachfläche ist nahezu vollständig mit monokristallinen Fotovoltaik-Modulen belegt.

R6, Königswinter
R6, Königswinter

R6 enjoys a wonderful location on the Rhine. It sits facing a large garden at the front, and partly rests against the rear wall of an existing hotel at the back. The narrow side of R6 is only separated from the Rhine by a riverside road, permitting a wonderful view out over the river from the upper floor. From a design point of view, R6 – like H16 and S3 before it – is a three-body problem. A small building facing the riverside road and boasting a historically listed red sandstone facade had to be integrated into the new building. Werner Sobek designed the house to retain this street-side facade in a red sandstone-coloured cuboid. A large glass wall connects this first structure to a second cuboid, which is clad in anthracite-coloured cement panels. The male owner's office is located in the sandstone structure. The garage, swimming pool, sauna, recreation areas, and the female owner's office are housed in the anthracite form. Between the two – and separated from the garden by a generously sized glass facade – is an entrance hall from which a staircase and an elevator lead up to the floor above.

The upper storey is a 37.38 m long, 8.50 m wide, totally glazed cuboid which rests on top of the two structures on the ground floor. The upper storey bridges the entrance lobby with a span of up to 18.96 m. The bedrooms, the kitchen, the eating area, and the sofa zone are

R6 ist das „Haus am Rhein". Seine Vorderseite ist einem großen Garten zugewandt, die Rückseite lehnt sich teilweise direkt an die Rückwand eines bestehenden Hotels. Die Schmalseite von R6 ist nur durch eine Uferstraße vom Rhein getrennt, sodass man vom Obergeschoss aus einen wunderbaren Blick über den Fluss hat. Gestalterisch gesehen ist R6 – wie schon H16 und S3 – ein Drei-Quader-Problem. Ein kleines, der Uferstraße zugewandtes Gebäude mit einer denkmalgeschützten Fassade aus rotem Sandstein war in das neue Gebäude zu integrieren. Werner Sobek formte dieses Gebäude unter Beibehaltung der straßenseitigen Fassade in einen sandsteinroten Quader, der durch eine große gläserne Wand mit einem zweiten, mit anthrazitfarbenen Zementplatten verkleideten Quader verbunden ist. Im Sandsteinquader befindet sich das Büro des Hauseigentümers. Im Anthrazitquader sind die Garage, das Schwimmbad, Sauna und Ruheräume sowie das Büro der Hausherrin untergebracht. Dazwischen liegt – durch eine großzügige Glasfassade vom Garten abgetrennt – die Eingangslobby, von der aus eine Treppe und ein Aufzug in das Obergeschoss führen.

Das Obergeschoss ist ein 37,38 m langer und 8,50 m breiter, vollkommen verglaster Quader, der auf den beiden Quadern des Erdgeschosses aufliegt. Das Obergeschoss überspannt die Eingangslobby mit

View of the house from the opposite bank of the Rhine.
Ansicht des Hauses vom gegenüberliegenden Rheinufer.
Overleaf: The garden with its historic stock of trees was an important element of the design concept.
Nächste Seite: Der Garten mit seinem historischen Baumbestand war wichtiger Bestandteil des Entwurfskonzepts.
Following pages: View of the house's southern side.
Folgende Seiten: Blick auf die Südseite des Hauses.

The transparent facade creates a fluid transition between the living space and the garden.
Die transparente Fassade schafft einen fließenden Übergang zwischen Wohnraum und Garten.

all found in the upper storey. The latter provides access to the terrace with its spectacular view out over the Rhine. In terms of their volume, colour and the tactile qualities of their surfaces, the individual building structures have been coordinated very strongly with one another and the garden. A large tree directly in front of R6 has been retained, as have many other plants. The rest of the garden is home to an installation of 44 elements with quadratic footprints, each of which holds a water basin or a single variety of plant. The colours of the garden, the surrounding area, and the individual structures form a carefully harmonised whole.

All interior wall and ceiling surfaces were covered in a dull, matt white. The flooring in the lower storey was laid in local greywacke (a type of sandstone). This floor covering runs out under the glass wall to form a terrace outside. The flooring in the upper storey is also made of greywacke. The building is heated and cooled using a groundwater heat pump. The distribution of heating and cooling takes place via underfloor heating and radiant cooling panels. Cooling for the house is achieved with a passive cooling unit and makes use of the relatively low temperature of the groundwater. A ventilation system with heat recovery capabilities ensures the hygienic renewal of air. An exterior solar shield considerably reduces the cooling loads. Simulations were carried out

einer Spannweite von bis zu 18,96 m. Im Obergeschoss befinden sich die Schlafräume sowie Küche, Essbereich und Sofazone. Von letzterer aus tritt man auf die Terrasse, die einen spektakulären Blick über den Rhein bietet. Die einzelnen Baukörper wurden in ihrem Volumen, ihrer Farbigkeit und in den taktilen Qualitäten ihrer Oberflächen sehr stark aufeinander sowie auf den Garten abgestimmt. Ein großer, unmittelbar vor R6 stehender Baum wurde ebenso wie viele andere Pflanzen erhalten. Der Rest des Gartens wurde durch eine Installation aus 44 im Grundriss quadratischen Elementen, die jeweils ein Wasserbecken oder eine einzige Pflanzensorte enthalten, ergänzt. Die Farben des Gartens, der Umgebung und der einzelnen Bauteile bilden ein sorgfältig aufeinander abgestimmtes Ganzes. Im Innenraumbereich wurden alle Wand- und Deckenflächen in einem stumpfen Weiß ausgeführt. Der Bodenbelag des Erdgeschosses wurde in der örtlich vorzufindenden Grauwacke (eine Sandsteinart) ausgeführt. Dieser Bodenbelag zieht sich unter der Glaswand hindurch ins Freie und bildet dort eine Terrasse. Grauwacke bildet auch den Boden des Obergeschosses.

Beheizt und gekühlt wird das Gebäude mit einer Grundwasser-Wärmepumpe. Die Verteilung von Wärme und Kälte erfolgt über eine Fußbodenheizung und über Kühldecken. Die Kühlung erfolgt über eine

Site plan and southern elevation.
Lageplan und Ansicht von der Südseite.

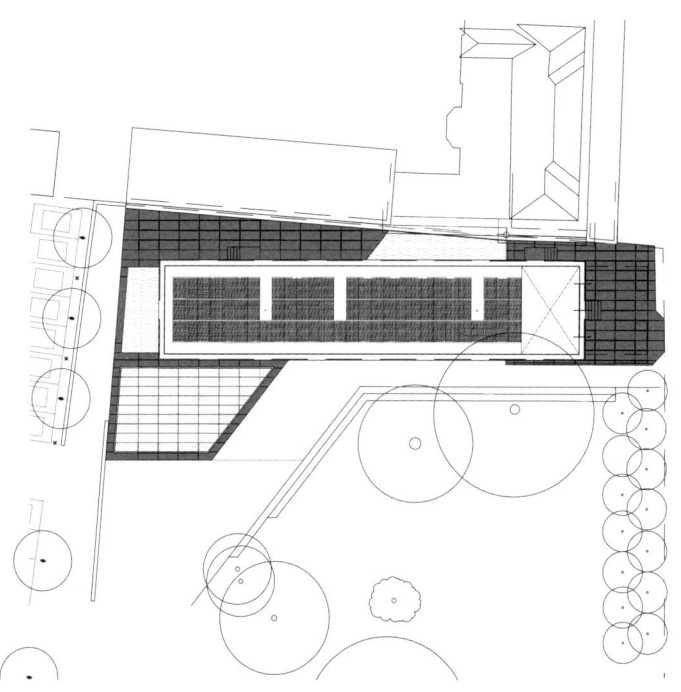

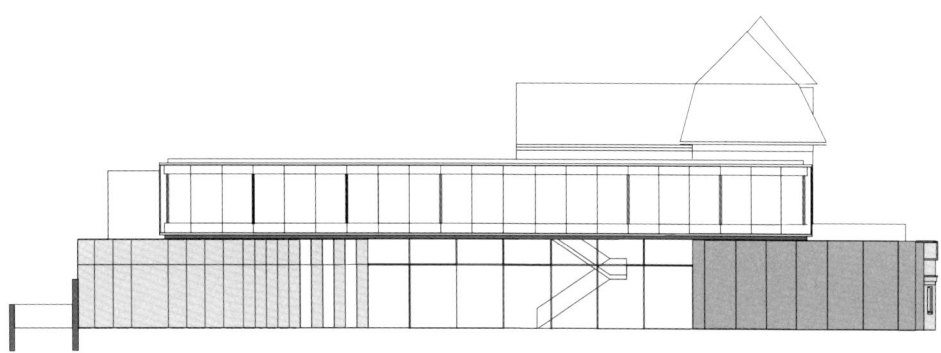

at a very early stage of the planning process to take into account the reduction in cooling loads due to the shade of the trees and neighbouring buildings.

passive Kühlstation und nutzt die relativ niedrige Temperatur des Grundwassers. Ein Lüftungsgerät mit Wärmerückgewinnung sorgt für einen hygienischen Luftwechsel. Ein außen liegender Sonnenschutz sorgt für eine deutliche Reduzierung der Kühllasten. Auch die Kühllastreduktion infolge der Verschattung durch Bäume und Nachbargebäude wurde mittels entsprechender Simulationen bereits zu einem sehr frühen Zeitpunkt in der Gebäudekonzeption berücksichtigt.

A staircase in the entrance area provides access to the upper storey.
Eine Treppe im Eingangsbereich dient der Erschließung des Obergeschosses.
Overleaf: The new building incorporates a historic structure – the male owner's office lies behind the sandstone facade.
Nächste Seite: Der Neubau integriert historische Bausubstanz – hinter der Sandsteinfassade liegt das Büro des Hausherrn.

Y1, Yssingeaux
Y1, Yssingeaux

Y1 lies in the raw landscape of the French Massif Central. The building is nestled harmoniously within its natural setting and offers breathtaking views of the surrounding volcanic landscape. The client and the architect found the building plot in a former open-pit sand mine after months of searching at the foot of a slope. The ground floor of the cellarless building is completely huddled down in the pit, making it only partially visible from the outside. As well as containing a reception and working area, the lower storey also houses a garage, a swimming pool, technical rooms, and two small self-contained apartments. All of these spaces are grouped around an interior courtyard which represents the central focal point of the completely inwardly orientated ground floor.

The upper storey, which takes the form of a glazed cuboid, sits slightly offset on top of the ground floor's flat roof. Its glazing affords magnificent views of the surrounding cones of extinct volcanoes – known locally as Les Sucs – as well as the herb garden and the terrace located on the slope. The upper storey contains the kitchen, the dining and living spaces, and the sleeping and sanitary areas. The ground and upper floors are connected by means of a staircase and an elevator.

In der rauen Landschaft des französischen Massif Central liegt Y1. Das Gebäude schmiegt sich harmonisch in die umgebende Natur ein und bietet atemberaubende Ausblicke auf die umgebende Vulkanlandschaft. Das Baugrundstück in Form einer ehemaligen Sandgrube fanden Bauherrschaft und Architekt nach monatelanger Suche am Fuße eines Hanges. Das Erdgeschoss des nicht unterkellerten Gebäudes schmiegt sich vollkommen in die Sandgrube ein, ist somit von außen nur zum Teil sichtbar. Das Erdgeschoss beherbergt neben einem Empfangs- und Arbeitsbereich auch eine Garage, einen Swimmingpool und Technikräume sowie zwei kleine Einliegerwohnungen. Alle diese Räume sind um einen Innenhof herum gruppiert, der den Mittelpunkt des vollständig nach innen konzentrierten Erdgeschosses darstellt.

Das Obergeschoss liegt, als gläserner Quader ausgeformt, leicht versetzt auf dem Flachdach des Erdgeschosses. Seine Verglasung eröffnet einen großartigen Blick auf die umgebenden Kegel erloschener Vulkane – die Sucs – sowie auf den Kräutergarten und die Terrasse, die an der Hangseite liegen. Das Obergeschoss beinhaltet den Schlaf- und Sanitärbereich sowie Küche, Ess- und Wohnbereich. Erdgeschoss und Obergeschoss sind durch eine Treppe sowie einen Aufzug miteinander verbunden.

Overleaf: The upper storey offers a sweeping view of the surrounding landscape which is characterised by its extinct volcanoes.
Nächste Seite: Aus dem Obergeschoss bietet sich ein weiter Blick auf die umgebende Landschaft, die von erloschenen Vulkanen geprägt ist.

Site plan – embedding the building complex into the flow of the landscape was an important hallmark of the design.
Lageplan – die Einbettung des Gebäudekomplexes in den Landschaftsverlauf war wichtiges Kennzeichen des Entwurfs.

114/115
Y1, Yssingeaux

Ground floor layout – the rooms are arranged around a central courtyard.
Grundriss des Erdgeschosses – die Räume sind um einen zentralen Innenhof herum angeordnet.

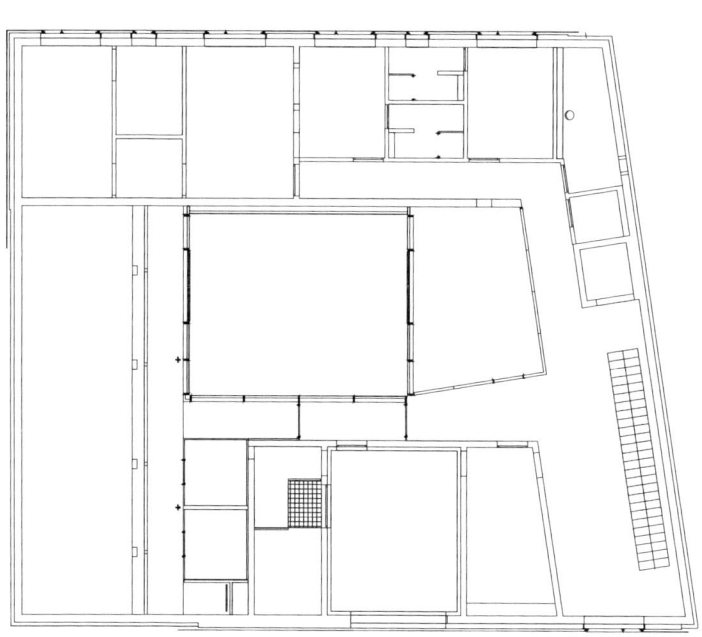

In a similar manner to H16, the steel-reinforced concrete structure of the ground floor is clad with black cement boards. The features of the lower storey – the matt black of the exterior shell; the carefully executed landscaping around the structure's downhill side; and the uphill, large format dry stone construction used to shore up the surrounding terrain – all serve to underscore the artistic objective of fully including – or, more precisely, integrating – the ground floor into the existing natural surroundings, an area that had previously suffered damage due to the open sand mine. Only the glazed cuboid of the upper floor is visible from the outside, i.e. from the nearby town or arterial roads. Thanks to its transparency, this second storey blends almost completely into its natural setting when seen from a distance.

Apart from the dark grey of the natural stone floor and a few areas of wall, all of the surfaces in the ground floor's interior are matt white. This reduced palette allows one's focus to be directed onto the colour of the interior courtyard, which is planted with a wide variety of local flowers and herbs. The surfaces in the upper floor are also matt white. As with the lower storey, the colour here comes exclusively from the tones of the natural surroundings.

Ähnlich wie H16 wurde das in Stahlbetonbauweise errichtete Erdgeschoss mit schwarzen Zementfaserplatten verkleidet. Das matte Schwarz dieser Außenhülle, die sorgfältig vorgenommenen talseitigen Anschüttungen an den Gebäudekörper sowie die hangseitige Abmauerung des anstehenden Geländes mittels großformatiger Steine in Trockenbauweise – all diese Faktoren unterstreichen die gestalterische Intention der vollständigen Einbindung, ja Integration des Erdgeschosses in die vorgefundene, durch die Sandgrube einstmals verletzte Natur. Einzig und allein der gläserne Quader des Obergeschosses ist von außen, das heißt von der nahe gelegenen Stadt oder den Ausfallstraßen her, sichtbar. Dank seiner Transparenz verschwimmt das Obergeschoss aus weiterer Entfernung jedoch nahezu vollständig mit der umgebenden Natur.

Alle Oberflächen im Erdgeschoss sind in mattem Weiß gehalten; nur die Natursteinböden und wenige Wandflächen sind dunkelgrau. Diese reduzierte Farbgebung ermöglicht eine Fokussierung auf die Farbigkeit des Innenhofs, der mit einer Vielzahl von Blumen und Kräutern aus der Region versehen ist. Die Oberflächen im Obergeschoss sind ebenso in einem matten Weiß gehalten. Wie im Erdgeschoss entsteht auch hier Farbigkeit ausschließlich durch die Farben der umgebenden Natur.

The two storeys are connected by a staircase and an elevator.
Die beiden Geschosse sind durch eine Treppe und durch einen Aufzug miteinander verbunden.
Overleaf: View of Les Sucs from the living and dining area.
Nächste Seite: Blick aus dem Wohn- und Essbereich auf die umgebenden Sucs.
Following pages: The building's location, embedded in a former open-pit sand mine, is revealed to visitors as they arrive. In a similar manner to H16, glass, concrete and natural stone are used in equal measure to shape the exterior space.
Folgende Seiten: Die Einbettung in eine ehemalige Sandgrube erschließt sich dem Besucher bereits bei der Anfahrt. Ähnlich wie bei H16 finden auch hier Glas, Beton und Naturstein gleichermaßen Anwendung zur Gestaltung des Außenraums.

Aktivhaus B10, Stuttgart

Overleaf: The building is part of the 'Electromobility showcase' research association – as a result, it was consciously given an open facade facing the street.
Nächste Seite: Das Gebäude ist Bestandteil des Forschungsverbunds „Schaufenster Elektromobilität" – es öffnet sich deshalb bewusst zur Straßenseite hin.

Aktivhaus B10 is part of a research project which examines how innovative materials, constructions and technologies can improve our built environment in a sustainable manner. Thanks to a sophisticated energy concept and a predictive, self-learning building control system, the house produces twice as much energy from sustainable sources as it requires for its own needs. The surplus energy generated is used to power two electric cars and – utilising smart grid technology – a neighbouring building designed by the architect Le Corbusier (which has been home to the Weissenhof Museum since 2006). The combination of mobile and permanent infrastructures is an extremely promising approach for creating an integrated, decentralised power supply to serve the needs of both electromobility and the built environment.

Throughout the entire duration of the project, both the consumption and generation of energy and a wide variety of further data relevant to building research will be continually measured and scientifically evaluated at the Institute for Lightweight Structures and Conceptual Design (ILEK) at the University of Stuttgart. B10 is part of the 'Schaufenster LivingLab BWe mobil' project network which promotes around 40 schemes in the Stuttgart and Karlsruhe regions. The project is supported by the Federal Ministry of Transport and Digital Infrastructure in Berlin.

Das Aktivhaus B10 ist Teil eines Forschungsprojekts, in dem untersucht wird, wie innovative Materialien, Konstruktionen und Technologien unsere gebaute Umwelt nachhaltig verbessern können. Dank eines ausgeklügelten Energiekonzepts und einer vorausschauenden, selbstlernenden Gebäudesteuerung erzeugt das Gebäude das Doppelte seines Energiebedarfs aus nachhaltigen Quellen. Mit dem gewonnenen Überschuss werden zwei Elektroautos und – im Rahmen eines Smart Grid (intelligenten Stromnetzes) – ein benachbartes Gebäude des Architekten Le Corbusier (seit 2006 Heimat des Weißenhofmuseums) versorgt. Der Zusammenschluss von mobiler und immobiler Infrastruktur ist ein vielversprechender Lösungsansatz für eine integrierte und dezentrale Energieversorgung von Elektromobilität und gebauter Umwelt.

Während der gesamten Projektlaufzeit werden Verbrauch und Gewinnung von Energie sowie eine Vielzahl weiterer für die Gebäudeforschung relevanter Daten kontinuierlich gemessen und am Institut für Leichtbau Entwerfen und Konstruieren (ILEK) der Universität Stuttgart wissenschaftlich ausgewertet. B10 ist Teil des Projektverbunds „Schaufenster LivingLab BWe mobil", in dem rund 40 Projekte in den Regionen Stuttgart und Karlsruhe gefördert werden. Das Projekt wird unterstützt vom Bundesministerium für Verkehr und digitale Infrastruktur, Berlin. Die

The building's timber structure is protected from the elements by a textile covering – an important feature which allows the building to be fully dismantled at the end of its life cycle.

Stuttgart, the state capital, has made a plot of land belonging to the city available for three years to allow the project to be carried out. Like most of the research buildings designed by Werner Sobek, B10 uses a minimum of resources and is fully recyclable. It thus fulfils all of the requirements of the Triple-Zero standard: the building generates more energy than it needs (zero energy), creates no emissions whatsoever (zero emissions) and can be reintroduced into the materials cycle without leaving any residual waste (zero waste).

The building plot is found in Bruckmannweg 10 at the heart of Stuttgart's famous Weissenhof Estate (called the 'Weißenhofsiedlung' in German). In the 1920s, this estate was a groundbreaking beacon for essential improvements to our built environment. Situated on the Killesberg hills, Aktivhaus B10 adopts the innovative spirit of the development and takes it into new realms – realms in which real estate and mobility are conceived of and designed as an integral unit. B10 dovetails the energy systems of electromobility and buildings to form an overarching, integral control system. It thus combines the charging infrastructure and the building services equipment used for the generation, storage and management of energy into a central unit – making B10 the link between the user, the building, the vehicle, and the smart grid.

Die Holzkonstruktion des Gebäudes wird durch eine Textilbespannung vor der Witterung geschützt – wichtige Voraussetzung für einen sortenreinen Rückbau am Ende des Lebenszyklus.

Landeshauptstadt Stuttgart hat für die Realisierung des Projekts das im städtischen Eigentum stehende Grundstück für drei Jahre zur Verfügung gestellt. B10 ist wie die meisten von Werner Sobek entworfenen Forschungsgebäude ressourcenminimal und vollkommen rezyklierbar. Es erfüllt somit alle Anforderungen des Triple-Zero-Standards: Das Gebäude erzeugt mehr Energie, als es selbst benötigt (zero energy), verursacht keinerlei Emissionen (zero emissions) und kann ohne Rückstände in den Stoffkreislauf rückgeführt werden (zero waste).

Das Baugrundstück befindet sich im Bruckmannweg 10, im Herzen der berühmten Stuttgarter Weißenhofsiedlung. Diese war in den 1920er-Jahren bahnbrechendes Signal für essenzielle Neuerungen in unserer gebauten Umwelt. Das Aktivhaus B10 am Killesberg greift diesen Innovationscharakter auf und überführt ihn in neue Bereiche – Immobilien und Mobilität werden als eine integrale Einheit gedacht und konzipiert. B10 verzahnt die Energiesysteme von Elektromobilität und Gebäuden zu einem integral gesteuerten Gesamtsystem. Es vereint somit die Ladeinfrastruktur und die Anlagentechnik für die Erzeugung, die Speicherung und das Management von Energie in einem zentralen Element – B10 wird hierdurch zum Bindeglied zwischen Nutzer, Gebäude, Fahrzeug und Smart Grid.

Due to its understated volume, its simple cubic design and its pared-down, white-focused colour scheme, Aktivhaus B10 blends perfectly into the listed Weissenhof Estate. With its technology, its high residential quality and its outstanding sustainable attributes, B10 picks up the ideas and objectives of classic modernism and guides them on into the 21st century.

As well as its energy efficiency, the building also offers some important constructional innovations. B10 was designed and industrially prefabricated as a timber structure within the space of a few months before being assembled on-site in just one day. One example of the building's diverse structural innovations is the use of vacuum glazing just 17 mm thick, which the B10 project has implemented for the very first time in the form of a storey-high glass facade. Further important advances include the installation of a prefabricated technical unit with a central cable harness, as well as fold-down facade elements (which fulfil a dual function as a terrace) and a fully recyclable timber-and-textile wall construction, etc.

The building itself was created as a highly insulated timber panel construction. To guarantee perfect recyclability, the timber components were neither painted nor coated in any way. For the same reason, it was

Aktivhaus B10 fügt sich durch sein zurückgenommenes Volumen, seine einfache Kubatur und seine auf Weiß reduzierte Farbigkeit perfekt in die denkmalgeschützte Weißenhofsiedlung ein. In seiner Technologie, seiner hohen Nutzungsqualität und den überragenden Nachhaltigkeitsqualitäten nimmt B10 die Ideen und Ziel der klassischen Moderne auf und führt sie weiter in das 21. Jahrhundert.

Das Gebäude bietet neben seiner Energieeffizienz auch wichtige konstruktive Neuerungen. B10 wurde innerhalb weniger Monate geplant und industriell als Holzbau vorgefertigt und dann innerhalb eines Tages vor Ort montiert. Zu den diversen baulichen Innovationen des Gebäudes zählt z. B. der Einsatz eines nur 17 mm dicken Vakuumglases, das bei B10 erstmals in Form einer geschosshohen Verglasung eingesetzt wurde. Weitere wichtige Innovationen sind die Installation einer vorgefertigten Technik-Einheit mit zentralem Leitungsbaum, klappbare Fassadenelemente (die eine Doppelfunktion als Terrasse erfüllen), eine voll rezyklierbare Holz-Textil-Wandkonstruktion etc.

Das Gebäude selbst wurde in einer hoch wärmegedämmten Holztafelbauweise ausgeführt. Die Holzbauteile wurden weder gestrichen noch anderweitig beschichtet, um so eine perfekte Rezyklierbarkeit zu gewährleisten. Auf Außenputz – d. h. ein Bestandteil des Gebäudes,

Integrating electromobility into the building was an important element of the design concept.
Die integrale Einbindung der Elektromobilität in das Gebäude war wichtiger Bestandteil des Entwurfskonzepts.
Overleaf: The extensive glazing on the west facade can be opened to permit quick, natural ventilation.
Nächste Seite: Die großflächige, öffenbare Verglasung auf der Westseite erlaubt eine schnelle natürliche Belüftung.
Following page: The terraces can be raised as required to provide an optical and thermal barrier.
Übernächste Seite: Die Terrassen können bei Bedarf hochgeklappt werden und dienen so als optische und thermische Barriere.

necessary that the use of exterior rendering – a constructional component that usually consists of several layers of irreversibly combined building materials and coating systems – also be avoided. An open mesh fabric was therefore stretched in front of the exterior walls. This allows the surface of the timber to be ventilated, provides shade and keeps insects at bay while simultaneously also ensuring that the exterior walls do not become wet when it rains.

The building's structure is completely closed on three sides. The west facade consists of four wall elements that can be folded down. In their closed (upright) state, these highly insulated panels enclose the entire building, thus guaranteeing a maximum of thermal insulation. When opened (folded down), the west facade forms a terrace and provides access to the building. The building's electric Smart vehicles can also drive over this entrance area. This makes it possible for an electric car to navigate directly into the residential space, allowing it to be charged and discharged right within the living quarters itself. As the electric Smart car comes to a halt on a turntable, it can be rotated to face any desired direction inside the house. This not only serves to improve user comfort, but also enhances the building's accessibility for people with disabilities.

das üblicherweise aus mehreren Lagen miteinander unlösbar verbundener Baustoffe und Anstrichsysteme besteht – sollte aus Gründen der Rezyklierbarkeit verzichtet werden. Vor die Außenwände wurde deshalb ein offenes Gittergewebe gespannt. Dieses erlaubt eine Belüftung der Holzoberfläche, wirkt schattierend, hält Insekten fern und sorgt gleichzeitig dafür, dass die Außenwandoberflächen bei Regen nicht nass werden.

Der Baukörper ist auf drei Seiten vollständig geschlossen. Die Westfassade besteht aus vier nach unten klappbaren Wandelementen. Im hochgeklappten Zustand schließen die hoch wärmegedämmten Wandelemente das gesamte Gebäude ein und garantieren so eine maximale Wärmedämmung. Die Westfassade bildet im heruntergeklappten Zustand eine Terrasse sowie den Zugang zum Gebäude. Der Zugangsbereich ist auch mit dem zum Gebäude gehörenden Elektro-Smart befahrbar. Das Elektrofahrzeug kann so in die Wohnung einfahren, was ein Be- und Entladen unmittelbar in der Wohnung erlaubt. Dadurch, dass das Fahrzeug auf einem drehbaren Bodenelement zum Stehen kommt, kann der Elektro-Smart innerhalb der Wohnung in jedwede Position gedreht werden. Dieser Ansatz dient nicht nur dem Nutzerkomfort, sondern trägt auch zu einem barrierefreien Bauen bei.

The moveable interior walls are also covered with fabric.
Auch die versetzbaren Innenwände sind mit einer Textilverkleidung versehen.

The kitchen facilities, shelving and storage space are located behind the wooden panelling.

Die Kücheneinrichtung befindet sich ebenso wie Regale und Stauraum hinter der Holzvertäfelung.

A significant feature of B10's interior is its high level of functional flexibility. All of the dividing walls are mobile, allowing the house to fulfil its functions as an information centre and a living and working space in the best possible way. All of the access doors and doors integrated into the dividing walls are sliding constructions. The sanitary and kitchen areas were delivered as prefabricated units and installed following the 'Plug and Play' principle. Each of the interior surfaces (including the floors) can thus easily be changed or exchanged, allowing them to be adapted to suit various types of use.

B10's energy concept is intended to generate around 200 per cent of its own energy requirements from renewable sources. A condition for reaching this goal is attaining a high level of thermal performance from the building envelope and fulfilling heating and cooling requirements in a manner that is both very efficient and conserves resources. The result is that very little primary energy is used to attain a comfortable interior temperature. The building is warmed by means of a heat pump which uses an ice storage tank and a photovoltaic array as thermal sources. This solution makes high efficiency ratios possible and, as a result, provides an efficient supply of heat for the house. The building is cooled via the ice storage tank – the ice used for this purpose in summer is

Der Innenraum von B10 ist von einer hohen Nutzungsflexibilität gekennzeichnet. Um die Funktionen Info-Zentrum, Wohnen und Arbeiten bestmöglich erfüllen zu können, wurden alle Trennwände als verschiebbare Wände konstruiert. Alle Zugangstüren sowie die in die Trennwände integrierten Türen sind Schiebetüren. Der Sanitärbereich wie der Küchenbereich wurden als vorgefertigte Einheiten angeliefert und nach dem „Plug-and-Play"-Prinzip eingebaut. Alle Oberflächen des Innenraums (einschließlich der Fußböden) können so auf einfache Weise verändert oder ausgetauscht werden. Die Innenraumoberflächen können somit, falls erforderlich, unterschiedlichen Nutzungsarten angepasst werden.

Das Energiekonzept von B10 sieht eine ca. 200-prozentige Deckung des eigenen Energiebedarfs aus erneuerbaren Quellen vor. Voraussetzung für das Erreichen dieses Ziels ist eine hohe thermische Qualität der Gebäudehülle und eine sehr effiziente und ressourcenschonende Bereitstellung von Wärme und Kälte. Daraus ergibt sich ein sehr geringer Primärenergieverbrauch für den thermischen Komfort im Innenraum. Das Gebäude wird mittels einer Wärmepumpe beheizt, die auf einen Eisspeicher und eine PVT-Anlage als Wärmequelle zurückgreift. Diese Lösung ermöglicht hohe Arbeitszahlen und somit auch eine effiziente Wärmeversorgung des Gebäudes. Die Kühlung des Gebäudes erfolgt

The technical building services equipment is directly accessible from the living space and was consciously designed to be part of the interior.

Die technische Gebäudeausstattung ist direkt vom Wohnbereich aus zugänglich und wird bewusst als Teil des Interieurs inszeniert.

built up during the period when heating is necessary in winter. The only additional energy required for cooling purposes is the electricity needed to run the circulator pump; this power is generated directly on-site by the photovoltaic system. It is possible to thermally activate the floor and ceiling surfaces to create a pleasant interior climate (with low inlet temperatures). An innovative system concept with an integrated hydraulic matrix opens up extremely promising possibilities regarding the management of sources and sinks in the building.

über einen Eisspeicher – hierfür wird im Sommer das Eis verwendet, das während der Heizperiode im Winter entsteht. An zusätzlicher Energie für die Kühlung muss nur noch der Strom für die Umwälzpumpe eingebracht werden; dieser Strom wird über die Fotovoltaik-Anlage direkt vor Ort erzeugt. Fußboden- und Deckenflächen können thermisch aktiviert werden, um (mit niedrigen Vorlauftemperaturen) eine angenehme Innenraumtemperatur zu erzeugen. Ein neuartiges Anlagenkonzept mit integrierter Hydraulikmatrix eröffnet vielversprechende Möglichkeiten im Quellen- und Senken-Management des Gebäudes.

Aktivhaus B10, Stuttgart

Ground plan with furnishings for residential use.
Grundriss mit Möblierung für die Zeit der Wohnnutzung.
Installing the building services module, 16th May, 2014.
Installation des Technik-Moduls am 16.05.2014.
Overleaf: The electric vehicle and the living quarters are separated from one another by a moveable interior wall – this allows the living area to be enlarged as required.
Nächste Seite: Wohnbereich und Elektrofahrzeug sind durch eine versetzbare Innenwand voneinander getrennt – bei Bedarf kann der Wohnbereich so vergrößert werden.

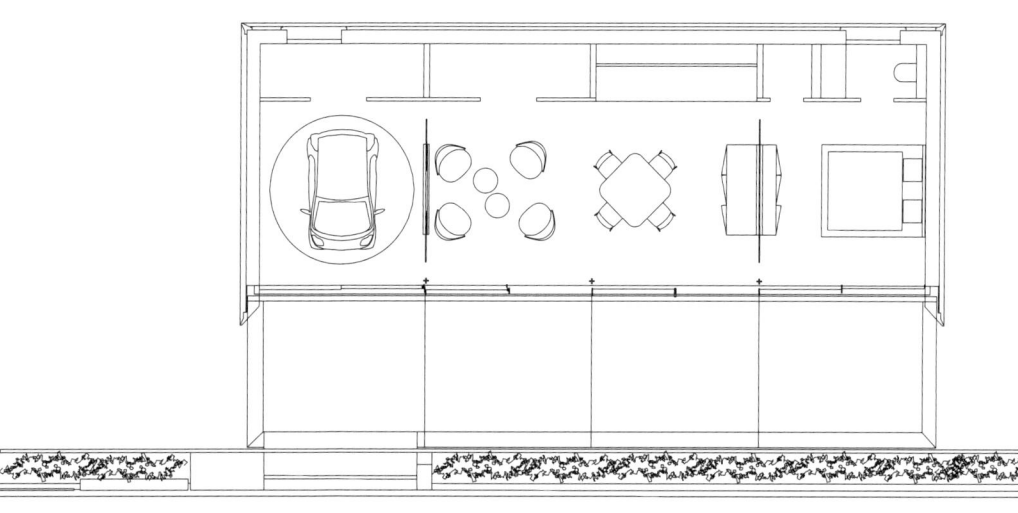

Aktivhaus B10, Stuttgart

Interview with Werner Sobek
Gespräch mit Werner Sobek

Thomas Geuder: Mr Sobek, you founded your company in 1992, at a time when ecological thinking and – to a greater extent – sustainable construction were still in their infancy. Nevertheless, there was already a certain pioneering spirit in the air back then. There was a great deal of excitement about 'experimental solar houses' at the International Horticultural Exposition IGA in Stuttgart, for example. Have the last 25 years taken place as you once dreamt they would? Or do you have to fall back on Karl Valentin's dictum, 'the future was also better in the past'?

Werner Sobek: Looking back, the last few decades have been lost years for the construction industry and society overall. We dismissed the many warnings from the Club of Rome and others far too quickly so we could plunge ourselves (at least in our society) into a culture of excess. At its height, this culture allowed the directors of banks to style themselves the unchallenged mediators of a divine will that gave the victor the right to all the spoils. Of course the whole affair was aided by political and intellectual elites turning a blind eye. A fatal mistake. It was not until the turn of the millennium that various reports from the United Nations clearly reminded the general public that the problems flagged up 40 years before were by then more relevant than ever. Today, we are witnessing the first harbingers of a population explosion in the form of

Thomas Geuder: Herr Sobek, Sie haben Ihr Unternehmen 1992 gegründet, also zu einer Zeit, als das ökologische Denken und erst recht das nachhaltige Bauen noch in den Kinderschuhen steckte. Dennoch war schon damals eine gewisse Aufbruchsstimmung zu spüren. Auf der IGA in Stuttgart z. B. schwärmte man von „experimentellen Solarhäusern". Sind die letzten 25 Jahre so verlaufen, wie Sie es sich damals erträumt haben? Oder muss man eher auf Karl Valentins Diktum zurückgreifen: „Früher war die Zukunft auch besser"?

Werner Sobek: Wenn man auf die letzten Jahrzehnte zurückblickt, dann waren es im Bauschaffen wie in der Gesellschaft insgesamt verlorene Jahrzehnte. Man hat die vielen Hinweise des Club of Rome und anderer viel zu schnell verdrängt, um sich (zumindest in unserer Gesellschaft) in eine Überflusskultur zu stürzen, auf deren Höhepunkt sich selbst Bankvorstände protestlos als Umsetzer göttlicher Überlegungen bezeichnen konnten, in der dem Sieger das Recht zugesprochen wurde, sich alles zu nehmen. Das Ganze war natürlich auch ein Wegsehen der politischen wie der intellektuellen Eliten. Ein fatales Wegsehen. Erst zu Anfang dieses Jahrtausends ist der breiten Öffentlichkeit durch verschiedene Berichte der Vereinten Nationen noch einmal deutlich vor Augen geführt worden, dass die vor 40 Jahren aufgezeigten Probleme

boat refugees in the Mediterranean. Europe is surrounded by war zones, and the surveillance of our personal data by domestic and foreign secret services is quietly being accepted by politicians and the judiciary. Furthermore, we have become utterly apolitical, and have neither a stance on, nor a solution to, all of these problems.

Over the past decades, the construction industry has focussed its research too heavily on new buildings (and predominantly, in so doing, on the refinement of known methods). Nothing truly new has been developed. Investigation into how to handle the large mass of existing structures or create a home for the exploding population has been neglected. Admittedly, other countries have done even less; but that is no excuse. Despite all this, I would like to remain optimistic and say: we have recognised the problem, now we must tackle it with all our collective force. We must do this with the highest levels of accuracy, quality, and care in dealing with nature. It is self-evident that technology will be used to this end. As a researcher, I will happily admit here that my interest in combining environmental protection and technology is not solely based on my suspicion that it will yield a large part of the solution – it is also a great source of academic fascination for me personally.

aktueller sind denn je. Heute erleben wir die ersten Vorboten der Bevölkerungsexplosion in Form der Bootsflüchtlinge im Mittelmeer. Europa ist von Kriegsgebieten eingekreist, die Überwachung unseres persönlichen Datenraumes durch eigene wie ausländische Geheimdienste wird von Politik und Justiz schweigend hingenommen. Und wir sind vollkommen apolitisch geworden, haben keine Haltung zu bzw. keine Lösungen für alle diese Probleme.

Das Bauwesen hat in den vergangenen Jahrzehnten den Fokus seiner Forschungen zu stark auf den Neubau (und dort zumeist auf die Verfeinerung bekannter Methoden) gelegt. Wirklich Neues wurde nicht entwickelt. Eine Forschung darüber, wie man mit der großen Masse der Bestandsbauten umgehen oder wie man für die explosionsartig wachsende Bevölkerung Heimat schaffen könnte, wurde vernachlässigt. Zugegeben: Andere Länder haben noch weniger getan; das ist aber keine Begründung. Dennoch möchte ich Optimist bleiben und sage: Wir haben das Problem erkannt, jetzt müssen wir es mit aller Kraft gemeinsam anpacken. Das müssen wir mit höchster Akkuratesse, Qualität und Sorgfalt im Umgang mit der Natur tun. Der Einsatz von Technik ist hierbei selbstverständlich. Als Forscher gebe ich an dieser Stelle gerne zu, dass ich in der Verbindung aus Umweltschutz und Technologie nicht nur einen großen Teil der Lösungen vermute, sondern dass für mich hierin auch ein wissenschaftliches Faszinosum liegt.

TG: Do you think the construction industry has done enough to protect the climate?

WS: No, not by a long shot. We are not even using the right terminology or telling the right story in our society. We talk about the need to save energy, for instance. But we do not have an energy problem – we have a $CO_2$ problem! All we need to do is stop burning fossilised sources of energy. That is the only issue here. There is a surplus of what we call renewable energy. The sun shines 10,000 times more energy down on the earth than we require in total. If we could capture enough of it, we would not need to make our houses airtight or clad them with thick insulation. Our impure reasoning might lead to an enormously costly reduction in the overall consumption of energy, but it will not force us to stop exploiting fossil fuels. Using pellets, gas or oil to heat a low-energy house might diminish the amount of $CO_2$ produced, but it is still being emitted. And so we remain part of the problem.

This is also apparent in another aspect of the current construction industry. In accordance with scientific advice, politicians have given us a target figure for energy saving measures that stipulates a maximum level of energy consumption per square metre of living space. They have also specified exactly how this goal should be attained. In doing so,

TG: Denken Sie, dass im Bauwesen genug für den Klimaschutz getan wurde?

WS: Nein, noch lange nicht. Wir verwenden in unserer Gesellschaft noch nicht einmal die richtigen Begrifflichkeiten, zeichnen nicht die richtigen Bilder. Wir sprechen beispielsweise von der Notwendigkeit, Energie einzusparen. Wir haben jedoch kein Energieproblem – wir haben ein $CO_2$-Problem! Es geht lediglich darum, dass wir keine fossilen Energieträger mehr verbrennen. Nur das ist das Problem. Die sogenannten erneuerbaren Energien gibt es im Überfluss. Die Sonne strahlt 10.000-mal mehr Energie auf die Erde ein, als wir insgesamt benötigen. Würden wir genügend davon ernten, bräuchten wir unsere Häuser weder luftdicht machen noch sie mit dicken Wärmedämmpaketen einhüllen. Durch die Unsauberkeit in der Argumentation reduziert man zwar mit einem enormen Aufwand den Energieverbrauch insgesamt, erzwingt aber nicht den Verzicht auf fossil basierte Energie. Wer in seinem Niedrigenergiehaus mit Pellets, Gas oder Öl heizt, emittiert zwar weniger $CO_2$, aber er emittiert immer noch. Und er bleibt damit Teil des Problems.

Das zeigt sich auch bei einem anderen Aspekt des aktuellen Bauschaffens. Auf Anraten der Wissenschaft gibt die Politik eine Zielgröße für Energieeinsparmaßnahmen vor, die den maximalen Energie-

they have unfortunately forgotten that enforcing obligatory targets while simultaneously dictating the ways in which they should be achieved is an excellent strategy for inhibiting innovation ... Instead of concentrating on exclusively powering our buildings with renewable energy, we are busy meeting narrow standards. Although these rigid rules have been eased somewhat in recent times, they have not been relaxed enough in my opinion. And the years we have lost in this way mean we do not have the necessary technology at our disposal today.

Nevertheless, as Peter Sloterdijk once said, 'It is a fundamental human characteristic that people who are confronted with problems that are too difficult for them cannot leave them alone, despite their difficulty'. We should take that to heart. Tackling the problems that lie before us with immediacy and comprehensiveness is the only chance humanity has. I act accordingly.

TG: Mr Sobek, you advocate design principles in your role as an architect; as an engineer, you dedicate yourself to construction; as a university professor, you research what is possible tomorrow (and investigate how much sense it makes within the broader context of sustainability). You obviously have several hearts beating within you. Which beats the loudest?

verbrauch pro Quadratmeter Wohnraum vorschreibt. Gleichzeitig wird genau festlegt, wie dieses Ziel zu erreichen ist. Leider hat man dabei vergessen, dass die zwingende Verbindung von Zielsetzung und umzusetzenden Maßnahmen eine exzellente Strategie zur Verhinderung von Innovation ist ... Anstatt uns darauf zu konzentrieren, unsere Gebäude ausschließlich mit erneuerbarer Energie zu betreiben, werden punktuelle Maßnahmen getroffen. Mittlerweile wurden die genannten starren Regeln zwar etwas aufgeweicht, meines Erachtens jedoch nicht genug. Und die dadurch verlorenen Jahre bewirkten, dass wir heute nicht über die erforderlichen Technologien verfügen.

Dennoch: Peter Sloterdijk hat einmal gesagt: „Es gehört zur Signatur der Humanitas, dass Menschen vor Probleme gestellt werden, die für Menschen zu schwer sind, ohne dass sie sich vornehmen könnten, sie ihrer Schwere wegen unangefasst zu lassen." Dies sollten wir uns zu Herzen nehmen. Das sofortige und umfassende Angehen der vor uns liegenden Probleme ist die einzige Chance, die die Menschheit hat. Also handle ich entsprechend.

TG: Herr Sobek, als Architekt vertreten Sie gestalterische Grundsätze, als Ingenieur widmen Sie sich der Konstruktion, als Hochschullehrer erforschen Sie, was morgen machbar ist (und wie sinnvoll dies im

WS: (laughs) Definitely that of the designer. For me, everything I do as an academic or engineer is directed towards expanding the keyboard that allows me to play certain melodies. These melodies are my architecture. Ideally, people will be able to identify with my creations in a positive way. What is particularly important to me in this respect is non-visual architecture – the architecture of tactile, olfactory and acoustic properties. All of these things – touching, smelling, hearing – need to come together to create a whole. Over the space of many years, I have assembled a keyboard that allows me to develop a variety of different things with materialities, colours, difficult mathematical processes, optimisation techniques, and the most complicated of construction methods, etc. This puts me in a position to compose and perform whole musical scores together with my team. These scores are our buildings. This is what I find most fulfilling.

TG: You recognised early on in your career that there is a great need for action at the interfaces between disciplines. What makes working at these intersections so exciting for you personally?

WS: I like wandering through terra incognita. Of course, exploring the white spaces on the map of knowledge always comes with the risk of failure – but that does not frighten me. Uncharted regions contain great

Gesamtzusammenhang der Nachhaltigkeit ist). In Ihrer Brust schlagen also offensichtlich mehrere Herzen. Welches schlägt am stärksten?

WS: (lacht) Sicher das des Gestalters. Für mich ist das, was ich als Wissenschaftler oder als Ingenieur tue, nichts anderes als das Ausbauen einer Klaviatur, die es mir ermöglicht, bestimmte Melodien zu spielen. Diese Melodien sind die Architektur, mit der sich die Menschen im Idealfall positiv identifizieren. Besonders wichtig ist mir dabei die nichtvisuelle Architektur, also die Architektur der taktilen, olfaktorischen und akustischen Qualitäten. All diese Dinge – das Tasten, Riechen, Hören – müssen zusammen kommen, um ein Ganzes zu schaffen. Ich habe mir über viele Jahre hinweg eine Klaviatur zusammengebaut, die es mir ermöglicht, mit Materialitäten, Farbigkeiten, schwierigen mathematischen Prozessen, Optimierungsverfahren und kompliziertesten Konstruktionsmethoden etc. ganz unterschiedliche Dinge zu erarbeiten. Zusammen mit meinem Team versetzt mich dies auch in die Lage, ganze Partituren zu schreiben und zu spielen: Die Partituren, die unsere Gebäude sind. Das ist das, was mich am meisten erfüllt.

TG: Sie haben in Ihrer Laufbahn schon früh erkannt, dass es an den Schnittstellen zwischen den Disziplinen einen großen Handlungsbedarf gibt. Was macht für Sie persönlich diese Schnittstellenarbeit so spannend?

treasures and, most likely, hold a large part of the solution. There is also an intellectual enrichment that comes from stepping over the boundaries of disciplines. Even at the start of my studies, I could not understand why structural engineers learnt to analyse at university, but never ventured into synthesis. That is why I also went to other faculties' lectures on architecture, textile engineering, vehicle bodywork construction, and aircraft manufacture, for example. I tried to learn within very different fields so that I would end up being able to create what was important to me. One naturally has to accept that moving between disciplines always puts one on uncertain terrain. Such movement constitutes the inner tension of my being, caught between extremely scientific work and research on the one hand, and the often entirely emotional momentum of design on the other. But do not worry: it is manageable.

TG: There is doubtless always also a need to transcend the boundaries formed by the current state of technology. What is your next goal in this regard?

WS: I am now in the fortunate position of having attained what I once set out to do. I have even achieved more than I imagined – as a result, I am content. I am not talking about my 'career' here; all that interests me is substance. I always like to stress that the proper pronoun

WS: Mich interessiert das Wandern in der Terra incognita. Mit dem Erforschen der weißen Flecken auf der Landkarte des Wissens ist natürlich immer auch ein Risiko des Scheiterns verbunden – was mich aber nicht schreckt. In den bislang noch nicht erforschten Bereichen ruhen große Schätze und wahrscheinlich ein großer Teil der Lösungen. Hinzu kommt die intellektuelle Bereicherung, die durch ein Überschreiten der Disziplinengrenzen erfolgt. Schon am Anfang meines Studiums habe ich nicht verstanden, warum Bauingenieure an der Hochschule zwar lernen zu analysieren, jedoch nie zur Synthese übergehen. Deshalb bin ich auch zu Vorlesungen in anderen Fakultäten gegangen, wie etwa zur Architektur, zur Textiltechnik, zum Karosseriebau oder zum Flugzeugbau. Ich habe in ganz verschiedenen Bereichen zu lernen versucht, um so schließlich das kreieren zu können, was für mich wichtig ist. Dass man sich beim Bewegen zwischen den Disziplinen immer auf unsicherem Terrain befindet, muss man dabei natürlich akzeptieren. Das bildet den inneren Spannungsbogen meiner Person: zwischen dem gestalterischen, häufig vollkommen emotionalen Momentum und dem extrem wissenschaftlichen Arbeiten und Forschen. Aber keine Sorge: das ist machbar.

TG: Es ist sicherlich immer wieder auch ein Überschreiten von Grenzen, die durch den aktuellen Stand der Technik gebildet werden. Was ist dabei Ihr nächstes Ziel?

is 'we' in such discussions – after all, I am only an initiator, a catalyst, someone who pushes and pulls, creates an itch and throws open doors. I could never have achieved everything without my wonderful team who have been with me for many years and with whom many fantastic products have been created.

When all is said and done, I would be lying if I claimed there were any one type of building that I still burned to create. I am much more interested in becoming even better in what we already do. To be successful in this, you need to be a skilled integrator with an ability to build bridges and establish connections. The key is to be able to act as a transmitter. That has proven itself to be a vital step in the right direction so far. Having a relatively consistent, diverse team is important in this respect. For that reason, we do not just have architects and engineers working with us, but also product designers, historians, religious scholars, aircraft manufacturers, mechanical engineers, ceramic engineers, and many more besides. There are almost no limits in this regard.

TG: Let us discuss your vision for the future of construction: what do you expect from the next generation of architects and planners?

WS: I hope no one simply copies me. That would worry me, as I have naturally made my mistakes and do not realise some things quickly

WS: Ich bin mittlerweile in der glücklichen Lage, dass ich das, was ich mir einmal vorgenommen habe, erreicht habe. Ich habe sogar mehr erreicht, als ich mir erträumt habe – also bin ich ein in mir glücklicher Mensch. Mir geht es hierbei aber nicht um die Karriere, sondern ausschließlich um das Inhaltliche. Dabei betone ich immer wieder gerne das „Wir", denn ich bin nur ein Initiator, ein Katalysator, jemand, der zieht und drückt, der Unruhe erzeugt und Türen aufstößt. All das könnte ich nie ohne das wunderbare Team leisten, das mich seit vielen Jahren begleitet und mit dem zusammen viele fantastische Produkte entstanden sind.

Schlussendlich müsste ich lügen, wenn ich sagen würde, es gäbe eine Art von Gebäude, das ich unbedingt noch machen möchte. Vielmehr will ich bei dem, was wir machen, noch besser werden. Hierfür braucht man eine Verknüpfungskompetenz, um Brücken schlagen und Verbindungen herstellen zu können. Es geht darum, als Transmitter wirken zu können. Das hat sich bisher als ein sehr wichtiger und richtiger Schritt erwiesen. Wichtig dabei ist eine relative Konstanz und Vielfältigkeit des Teams. So arbeiten bei uns nicht nur Architekten und Ingenieure, sondern auch Produktgestalter, Historiker, Religionswissenschaftler, Flugzeugbauer, Maschinenbauingenieure, Keramikingenieure und viele andere. Es gibt hier fast keine Beschränkungen.

enough. Nevertheless, I hope – no, I am sure – that my colleagues will find ways to continue and further develop my work. Responsible innovation can only come about if we tread new paths while following clear, unshakeable ethical principles. In the construction industry in particular, we must do everything imaginable to develop solutions that will remain sustainable for society and the environment in the future. To do this, we must also free ourselves from the cocoon of professional and legal rules and traditions that often too strongly influences our thought and action. We are regrettably on the road to becoming a 'fully insured society' – one in which people no longer accept any risk and are no longer allowed to make mistakes. We are unaware that this development is robbing us of an essential part of what it means to be human.

TG: Which questions and solutions are you currently working on?

WS: I yearn for a built environment in which people can live in happy, healthy harmony with nature for a reasonable price, using minimal resources and powered by solar energy. I can merely sketch out the path to that goal. I only know some of the barriers that still need to be overcome. My team and I have reached a point at which we have perfectly mastered the keyboard of sustainable building. For this, we have developed a structure, a form of organisation and communi-

TG: Lassen Sie uns über Ihre Sicht auf die Zukunft des Bauwesens sprechen: Was erwarten Sie von den Architekten und Planern der nächsten Generation?

WS: Ich hoffe, dass mich niemand einfach kopiert. Das würde mich sorgen, denn natürlich habe auch ich Fehler gemacht, erkenne manche Dinge nicht schnell genug. Ich hoffe aber, ja ich bin sicher, dass meine Mitarbeiterinnen und Mitarbeiter Wege finden, meine Arbeiten fortzusetzen und sie dabei weiterzuentwickeln. Nur durch das Beschreiten neuer Wege bei gleichzeitig klaren und unverrückbaren ethischen Grundsätzen kann verantwortbare Innovation entstehen. Gerade im Bauwesen müssen wir alles Erdenkliche tun, um Lösungsansätze zu entwickeln, die für die Gesellschaft und die Umwelt auch in Zukunft tragfähig sind. Hierfür müssen wir uns auch von dem Kokon aus beruflichen und gesetzlichen Vorschriften und Traditionen befreien, der unser Denken und Handeln häufig zu stark beeinflusst. Wir befinden uns leider auf dem Weg zu einer Vollkasko-Gesellschaft, in der keiner mehr ein Risiko eingehen will und in der niemand mehr einen Fehler machen darf. Und wir merken nicht, dass wir dabei eine wesentliche Qualität des Mensch-seins an sich verlieren.

TG: An welchen Fragestellungen und Lösungen arbeiten Sie zurzeit?

cation, and a way of thinking, acting and planning. Our task now is to contemplate future forms of production for larger edifices. We will certainly still stumble upon a variety of new problems in the process. It is probable that building in situ cannot be sustainable by definition. We are therefore working on new solutions that allow us to produce sustainable constructions in different versions and standards and with the quality and efficiency of industrial production. This principle is comparable with a 'platform strategy', something we are now transferring to the building industry. We are striving to create a house that is also a home, that needs no energy, causes no emissions, is fully recyclable, and offers a high standard of living – all while significantly undercutting current costs. The savings potential of our new approaches is tremendous.

TG: Last but not least: what actually drives Werner Sobek – the engineer, architect and university professor – onwards?

WS: The search for knowledge and understanding; the quest for beauty (which I suspect lies in nothingness). This and this alone has driven and drives me on. I only stop searching, questioning, thinking, and working when I have understood or developed something so fundamentally that I can explain it to anyone over the phone. Titles and academic honours sometimes used to motivate me in my younger years – I will

WS: Ich sehne mich nach einer gebauten Umwelt, in der die Menschen glücklich und gesund im Einklang mit der Natur leben können, zu vernünftigen Preisen, ressourcenminimal, mit solarer Energie versorgt. Den Weg dorthin kann ich nur skizzieren. Die Hindernisse, die noch überwunden werden müssen, kenne ich nur zum Teil. In meinem Team sind wir an einem Punkt angelangt, an dem wir die Klaviatur des nachhaltigen Bauens perfekt beherrschen. Wir haben uns hierfür eine Struktur, eine Organisations- und Kommunikationsform, eine Art zu denken, zu handeln und zu planen erarbeitet. Nun geht es darum, über zukünftige Produktionsformen für größere Strukturen nachzudenken. Dabei werden wir sicher noch auf diverse neue Probleme stoßen. Der Bau in situ kann wahrscheinlich erklärtermaßen nicht nachhaltig sein. Wir arbeiten deshalb an neuen Lösungen, die es uns erlauben, nachhaltige Konstruktionen mit industrieller Qualität und Wirtschaftlichkeit sowie in unterschiedlichen Ausführungsstufen zu realisieren. Dieses Prinzip lässt sich mit einer „Plattformstrategie" vergleichen, die wir nun in das Bauwesen überführen. Wir streben nach einem Haus, das Heimat ist, das keine Energie braucht, das keine Emissionen tätigt, das voll rezyklierbar ist und das einen hohen Wohnkomfort bietet – die bisherigen Kosten aber deutlich unterschreitet. Die Einsparpotenziale unserer neuen Ansätze sind gewaltig.

readily admit to that. But that is all behind me now. All that matters to me today is trying to understand things even better, implement them even more effectively, refine them even more rigorously, and design them even more successfully. In the process, I have observed that – after all that learning, practicing and making – my solutions and designs are becoming ever more simple. That makes me very happy – simplicity is the ultimate goal, after all.

TG: A fine closing remark! Many thanks for this conversation, Mr Sobek.

TG: Zu guter Letzt: Was treibt den Ingenieur, den Architekten und den Hochschullehrer Werner Sobek tatsächlich an?

WS: Die Suche nach Wissen und Verstehen, die Suche nach Schönheit, die ich im Nichts vermute. Nur dies trieb und treibt mich an. Ich höre erst auf zu suchen und zu fragen, nachzudenken, zu arbeiten, wenn ich etwas so grundlegend verstanden oder entwickelt habe, dass ich es jedermann am Telefon erklären könnte. In meinen jungen Jahren haben mich gelegentlich auch Titel und akademische Ehren angetrieben – das gebe ich gerne zu. Das aber habe ich hinter mir. Es geht mir immer nur darum, die Dinge noch besser zu verstehen, sie noch besser umzusetzen, sie noch konsequenter weiterzuentwickeln, sie noch besser zu gestalten. Dabei beobachte ich, dass meine Lösungen, meine Entwürfe nach all' dem Lernen, Üben, Machen immer einfacher werden. Hierüber bin ich sehr froh, denn Einfachheit ist das letzte Ziel.

TG: Ein schönes Schlusswort! Vielen Dank für das Gespräch, Herr Sobek.

**Imprint and Credits** Impressum und Bildnachweise

**Editor and Concept** Herausgeber und Konzeption:
Frank Heinlein
**Text** Text:
Frank Heinlein
**Design, Layout, and Typesetting** Gestaltung, Layout und Satz:
Zimmermann Visuelle Kommunikation, Stuttgart
**Based on a layout by** Auf Basis des Grundlayouts von:
büro uebele visuelle kommunikation, Stuttgart
**Images** Abbildungen:
René Müller, Stuttgart (2)
Tillmann Franzen, Düsseldorf (15)
Zooey Braun, Stuttgart (19-21, 25-31, 36-41, 43-47, 62-73, 76-77, 96-103, 107-109, 112-113, 117-123, 126-141, 143-145, 153, 158-159)
Werner Sobek, Stuttgart (22-23, 42, 56-57, 74-75, 83, 91, 104-105, 114-115, 142)
Pasi Toiviainen, Helsinki (32-33)
Arnulf Hettrich, Stuttgart (50-55, 58-59)
Ulrich Schwarz, Berlin (80-81, 87)
Matthias Koslik, Berlin (84-85, 88-89)
**Typeface** Schrift:
Futura T Book
**Paper** Papier:
UPM Fine SC 150 g
**Translation** Übersetzung:
Jon Andrews, Ormskirk, England
**Proofreading** Korrektorat:
ARS Armin Schüler, Waiblingen
**Repro** Repro:
Identicolor, Stuttgart
**Printing** Druck:
Offizin Scheufele Druck und Medien GmbH & Co.KG, Stuttgart
**Binding** Bindung:
Lachenmaier GmbH, Reutlingen

© 2015 Werner Sobek, Stuttgart

**Distribution** Vertrieb:
av edition GmbH, Senefelder Straße 109, 70176 Stuttgart
www.avedition.com, contact@avedition.com

ISBN 978-3-89986-235-5